GETTING AWAY WITH MURDER

AF624831

ALSO BY HERALDO MUÑOZ

A Solitary War:
A Diplomat's Chronicle of the Iraq War and Its Lessons

The Dictator's Shadow:
Life Under Augusto Pinochet

GETTING AWAY WITH MURDER

Benazir Bhutto's Assassination and the Politics of Pakistan

HERALDO MUÑOZ

W. W. NORTON & COMPANY

New York · London

Viva Books

New Delhi | Mumbai | Chennai | Kolkata | Bengaluru | Hyderabad | Kochi | Guwahati

Copyright © 2014 by Heraldo Muñoz

First Indian Edition 2014

VIVA BOOKS PRIVATE LIMITED

- 4737/23 Ansari Road, Daryaganj, New Delhi 110 002
  E-mail: vivadelhi@vivagroupindia.net, Tel. 42242200
- 76, Service Industries, Shirvane, Sector 1, Nerul, Navi Mumbai 400 706
  E-mail: vivamumbai@vivagroupindia.net, Tel. 27721273, 27721274
- Megh Tower, Old No. 307, New No. 165, Poonamallee High Road, Maduravoyal
  Chennai 600 095 E-mail: vivachennai@vivagroupindia.net, Tel. 23780991, 23780992
- B-103, Jindal Towers, 21/1A/3 Darga Road, Kolkata 700 017
  E-mail: vivakolkata@vivagroupindia.net, Tel. 22836381, 22816713
- 7, Sovereign Park Apartments, 56-58, K. R. Road, Basavanagudi, Bengaluru 560 004
  E-mail: vivabangalore@vivagroupindia.net, Tel. 26607409, 26607410
- 101-102 Mughal Marc Apartments, 3-4-637 to 641, Narayanguda, Hyderabad 500 029
  E-mail: vivahyderabad@vivagroupindia.net, Tel. 27564481, 27564482
- Beevi Towers, First Floor, SRM Road, Kaloor, Kochi 682 018, Kerala
  E-mail: vivakochi@vivagroupindia.net, Tel: 0484-2403055, 2403056
- 232, GNB Road, Beside UCO Bank, Silpukhuri, Guwahati 781 003
  E-mail: vivaguwahati@vivagroupindia.net, Tel: 0361-2666386

www.vivagroupindia.com

Published by arrangement with
W. W. Norton & Company, Inc.
500 Fifth Avenue, New York
N Y 10110

All rights reserved. No part of this book may be reproduced or utilized in any form or by any means, electronic or mechanical, including photocopying, recording or by any information storage or retrieval systems, without permission in writing from the publisher.

This edition is for sale in the India, Sri Lanka, Bangladesh and Nepal only. Not for export elsewhere.

ISBN : 978-81-309-2666-7

Published by Vinod Vasishtha for Viva Books Private Limited, 4737/23, Ansari Road, New Delhi-110 002. Printed and bound by Glorious Printers, Delhi.

To Pamela, my wife and partner,
and to my daughter Paloma

Contents

List of Illustrations

List of Illustrations

1. Benazir Bhutto at her 1988 swearing-in ceremony as prime minister (Alfred/Sipa Press)
2. Pakistan's first prime minister Liaquat Ali Khan meets US president Harry S. Truman (United States Department of State, courtesy of Harry S. Truman Presidential Library)
3. The Bhutto family (AP Photo)
4. The UN Commission at Benazir Bhutto's assassination site (Ken Dotzer/Malof)
5. US president George W. Bush and Pakistani president Pervez Musharraf (George W. Bush Presidential Library and Museum)
6. Benazir Bhutto returns to Pakistan after years of self-exile (Daniel Berehulak/Getty)
7. Dead and wounded at the assassination site (John Moore/Getty)
8. UN Commission meeting with Interior Minister Rehman Malik (The UN Commission of Inquiry)
9. Delivery of the UN Commission's final report to UN Secretary-General Ban Ki-moon (UN Photo/Mark Garten)

GETTING AWAY WITH MURDER

Preface

IN THE SOUTHERN-hemisphere summer of January 2009, while my wife and I vacationed in Chile at a cousin's home by a calm river near the town of Valdivia, I got an urgent call from the office of United Nations Secretary-General Ban Ki-moon in New York. His chief of staff, Ambassador Vijay Nambiar, transmitted a request from the secretary-general: Would I be able to lead a commission to investigate the assassination of former Pakistani prime minister Benazir Bhutto?

Nambiar said that Secretary-General Ban had agreed to constitute the commission at the request of the Pakistani government, presided over at that point by Benazir Bhutto's widower, Asif Ali Zardari. This commission would carry out an inquiry to shed light on the facts and circumstances of the former prime minister's murder and would not be an international tribunal with the obligation to establish criminal responsibilities. There would be two other high-level commissioners, yet to be determined, but the secretary-general wanted first to announce the creation of the commission and its chairperson.

I responded that I would have to consult the president of Chile,

Michelle Bachelet, as well as inform the foreign minister. It was highly unusual that a sitting ambassador to the UN would be entrusted with such a delicate duty. Generally, heads of UN commissions are *former* presidents, prime ministers, foreign ministers, or ambassadors. Nambiar requested a response as soon as possible.

I had serious doubts about accepting such high responsibility. The case looked like a lose-lose situation; any conclusion could leave many sides disappointed or even angry. I could not force anyone to testify, my powers would be limited, and public expectations would be high. Moreover, Pakistani political culture is characterized by rumors and conspiracy theories, as Pakistani writer Ali Sethi suggested in an essay about the terrorist attack in Lahore against the Sri Lankan national cricket team. While interviewing people in the street about the culprits, he was told that it could have been the work of "terrorists or criminals. . . . But it could be the agencies. It could be the government. It could be India also."[1]

I had visited the country and read about it, but I was far from being an expert, and I came from a nation geographically and culturally distant from Pakistan. Then, I reasoned, Chile did not have any hidden agenda, interests, or prejudices regarding Pakistan—a plus in the eyes of the UN and the Islamabad government. The task would be dangerous; but the secretary-general had probably taken into consideration, when offering me this challenge, that I had presided over the Al-Qaida and Taliban Sanctions Committee of the UN Security Council during 2003 and 2004.

President Bachelet reacted very positively when I consulted her on how to respond to the secretary-general's request. "It's a recognition of your personal trajectory and an honor for Chile," she said. "Go ahead and accept." I thus felt compelled to take on this difficult task.

Secretary-General Ban Ki-moon informed the Security Council on February 2, 2009, that, after consultations with members of the council and as requested by the government of Pakistan, he had decided to establish "an international commission in connection with the assassination on 27 December 2007 of former Prime Minister of Pakistan Mohtarma Benazir Bhutto." The commission, he stated, would be composed of "a panel of three eminent personalities having the appropriate experience and reputation for probity and impartiality." In an addendum, the secretary-general outlined the functioning conditions and responsibilities of the Commission of Inquiry.[2] In a letter dated February 3, the president of the Security Council "took note" of the decision of the secretary-general and made mention of the intention to "submit the report of the commission to the Security Council for information."[3]

On February 10, the secretary-general—having just returned from a trip that had taken him, among other places, to Afghanistan and Pakistan—announced that the UN commission to investigate the assassination of former prime minister Benazir Bhutto would be headed by me. Ban added that he had discussed the matter in Islamabad with President Zardari and Prime Minister Yousuf Gilani. My designation had leaked one week earlier when the ambassador of India to the United Nations, Nirupam Sen, had revealed to a news agency that I would lead the Commission of Inquiry.[4]

I recalled having met Benazir Bhutto in the early '90s, while I was ambassador to the Organization of American States (OAS), at a seminar on democratic transitions held in the US Congress. We were on the same panel; she spoke about Pakistan, and I gave a presentation on Chile. She was the star of the event and seemed poised and confident. We were able to chat for a while. I said that while doing my PhD at the Korbel

School of International Studies at the University of Denver, I had often discussed her father's 1977 military overthrow and arrest with my good Pakistani friend and classmate, Mustapha Kemal Pasha, who attended all the solidarity demonstrations that I organized against the Pinochet dictatorship and the 1973 coup that had overthrown Chilean president Salvador Allende. Benazir told me that Zulfikar Ali Bhutto admired Allende and knew perfectly well that the United States had plotted with rightists in Chile to oust his socialist government. The rest of our dialogue was a brief exchange of pleasantries during our respective lectures.

Now, almost twenty years later, I would lead the inquiry into the assassination of the charming and intelligent woman I had met at that seminar in Washington DC. I vaguely remembered having seen on TV a grainy video of the moment of her assassination. I had then thought that security must have lapsed, because I recalled her waving to a surrounding crowd without solid protection.

BENAZIR HAD NOT been born a politician. She had always wanted to be a diplomat and preferred intellectual debates to the corridors or smoked-filled rooms of power politics. But the killing of her father by the Zia ul-Haq dictatorship changed her. She became a determined daughter ready to take on the military dictator who had eliminated her father; in the process, she evolved into a political leader and inheritor of the Bhutto mantle. Benazir Bhutto became, per the title of her autobiography, a *Daughter of Destiny.* To be sure, she changed many more times in the coming years, twice becoming prime minister, facing exile, dealing with the realities of world politics, and negotiating with dictator Musharraf a deal to return home after more than a decade into her second exile.

Born on June 21, 1953, Benazir was also a daughter of fortune, the eldest of four children in a well-to-do family in the southern province of Sindh. Her English governess called her "Pinkie," as did the rest of her family, and at a young age Benazir enrolled in an elite Catholic school. English was her first language, her Urdu was less fluent, and she barely spoke any Sindhi. Her world opened up when she attended Radcliffe College and, in her words, was "forced . . . to grow up."[5] But Benazir was a woman of contradictions: modern-minded, with degrees from Harvard and Oxford, she accepted an arranged marriage to scale the ladder of power in the conservative political culture of Pakistan. One writer characterized her as "a feudal princess with the aristocratic sense of entitlement that came with owning great tracts of the country and the Western-leaning tastes that such a background tends to give."[6]

Benazir Bhutto was one of Pakistan's most important political figures, a respected world leader, and the leading stateswoman in the Islamic world. The West, despite occasional doubts about her abilities to govern, largely considered her a progressive figure who could advance the cause of democracy and counterterrorism in her native country. Bhutto was also hated and feared by many in Pakistan, particularly by the so-called "Establishment"—sections within the army and security services, certain businessmen, and Islamist extremists. They disliked and distrusted her popularity, her ties to the West, and her modernizing political agenda. Her political adversaries leveled accusations of corruption against her and her family, particularly her husband, Asif Ali Zardari, while the media and other skeptics criticized her lavish lifestyle.

Bhutto's murder occurred shortly after her return to Pakistan in the midst of an electoral campaign. The United States and Great Britain had facilitated her return. She knew that she was a security target but felt compelled to go back despite the dangers and despite the fact that her father, Zulfikar, and two brothers had died unnatural deaths. There was no shortage of people and groups in her home country that wanted Benazir Bhutto dead and had the power and means to eliminate her.

Against the backdrop of a Pakistani political history of unconsolidated democracy, betrayals, corruption, unsolved political assassinations, religious radicalism, and foreign influence—particularly that of the United States—Benazir returned in order to try, once again, to rally her people for the cause of democracy, secularism, and moderation. As a proud member of the Bhutto clan—a family that dates back to grandfather Sir Shahnawaz Bhutto, a Sindhi feudal lord who had been the *dewaan* (prime minister) of the state of Junagadh in the Indian colonial government before partition—she felt she had no other choice; it was her destiny and legacy to return to her homeland. Most observers believed Benazir would confront an insurmountable challenge in trying to restore democracy to Pakistan, and friends feared her days were numbered the moment she boarded that flight home from Dubai on October 17, 2007.

A FEW MONTHS after my designation as chairman of the Commission of Inquiry, the UN completed the team, naming two additional commissioners: former attorney general of Indonesia Marzuki Darusman and former deputy commissioner of the Irish Police Peter Fitzgerald. In the process of investigation, I became good friends with both of them, with our chief of staff, Mark Quarterman, and the analysts and other members of the team.

This book is based on the behind-the-scenes evidence and experiences we encountered during the yearlong inquiry, which culminated in the presentation of a report on April 15, 2010, which had an important international impact. This book makes abundant use of this report in chapters 7 and 8 but goes well beyond it, supplemented by my own extensive research into the assassination and its context and by my reflections on larger matters, like the US-Pakistan ties.

In fact, this book is as much about the Bhutto murder investigation as it is about the broader context of modern Pakistan and the critical US-Pakistani relationship. Benazir's tragic death is an entry point for a much bigger story: Pakistan's postindependence evolution and the influence of key outside actors, including the United States.

International media pointed to my background as an active opponent of dictator Augusto Pinochet in Chile, as well as my political and diplomatic trajectory, as a key factor behind my designation and as a component in producing what was seen as a substantive and unbiased report.[7] I would like to think that my experience prepared me to observe and penetrate the political and social context of Benazir Bhutto's assassination and to focus on the substantive drivers of the crime.

This book is an examination of political life and death in Pakistan—not just a look at the narrow subject matter or a treatment limited to statements by political actors. This is my personal view of the murder of Benazir Bhutto and her times and in no way compromises or necessarily reflects the views of the United Nations or those of the members of the Commission of Inquiry. This is a critical analysis of the assassination of a major political leader, her country, and her circumstances.

Benazir Bhutto on the occasion of her swearing-in as prime minister after her party won the largest bloc of seats in the National Assembly in the 1988 election. Her coalition government faced tensions with the army and with President Ghulam Ishaq Khan, leading to her dismissal in November 1990.

1

A Murder Foretold

IT WAS A warm afternoon on August 15, 2007, when Benazir Bhutto arrived at the Council on Foreign Relations building on East Sixty-Eighth Street and Park Avenue in Manhattan to give a public talk. It was an unusual meeting as the council rarely schedules activities in the lazy final month of the New York summer, but Bhutto drew a big audience interested in Pakistan and international affairs. Moreover, there was great eagerness to know her intentions. Many presumed she would return to her homeland after a long voluntary exile to lead a process of democratic reconstruction. Scholar and former US diplomat Richard Haass, the council's president, introduced Benazir with a personal touch, recalling that they had met thirty years ago at Oxford, where they had both studied. The former Pakistani prime minister was relaxed and amicable; she had prepared well for this occasion knowing that this was an important venue to speak on the record about her political plans to Pakistan and to the world.

Benazir began by tracing her country's troubles over the past half century, beginning with the first military takeover in 1958, and emphasizing that four military dictatorships had ruled her nation in the last thirty years. She wanted the public to understand the challenges of Pakistan: unconsolidated democracy, betrayals, corruption, political assassinations, socioeconomic inequality, foreign influence, and growing religious radicalism.

After her brief introduction, Benazir made a formal announcement to her US audience that was the product of months of reflection—an announcement that despite the opposition of many of her closest friends, mostly for security reasons, she felt obliged to carry through: "I plan to return this year to Pakistan," she said, "to lead a movement for the restoration of democracy. I seek to lead a democratic Pakistan which is free from the yoke of military dictatorship and that will cease to be a haven of international terrorism; a democratic Pakistan that would help to stabilize Afghanistan, relieving pressure on NATO troops; a democratic Pakistan that would pursue the drug barons and bust up the drug cartel that today is funding terrorism." Bhutto added that she would fight for "a democratic Pakistan that puts the welfare of its people at the centerpiece of its national policy" and closed her remarks reiterating her determination to confront the "forces of militancy and extremism."[1]

Benazir Bhutto had skillfully hit all the right notes for her attentive American audience. But a question during the Q&A period revealed some skepticism. Would she be able to tackle delicate issues that she had been incapable of solving during her two previous terms as prime minister? Her previous stints in office had been inconclusive, and the country had only become more complicated in the years since. Would an agreement of "political cohabitation" with ruling dictator General Pervez Musharraf work?

Yes, the challenges of Pakistan were formidable, Bhutto admitted, but was there a better option than her for a future of stability and democracy? As for the negotiations with Musharraf,

Benazir candidly explained that while agreements had been reached on several issues and he had "committed to taking certain confidence-building measures," tangible proof had not materialized. It remained to be seen, Benazir added, "if it is just talk or is it going to turn into a walk."[2]

Regarding her differences with Musharraf, Benazir postulated that there were "two fault lines: One between dictatorship and democracy, and the second between the forces of moderation and the forces of extremism." While one set of problems dealt with the unavoidable fact that Musharraf had been a coup leader, Benazir valued his declared intention to follow a moderate path so that moderate forces could "work together for a transition to democracy."[3] Bhutto complained that Musharraf did not want her to return to Pakistan before the scheduled December elections: "He says it will be destabilizing." But she dismissed this argument: going home might be "destabilizing to the ruling party," she said, "but it won't be destabilizing to the nation." Making reference to exiled leader Nawaz Sharif, who was also seeking to return to Pakistan, she added, "Elections cannot be free and fair unless the leaders of all parties are allowed to contest, and contest freely."[4]

About a month after her Council on Foreign Relations speech, Benazir Bhutto wrote in an op-ed in the *Washington Post* that she had decided to return to Pakistan after a long exile "to bring change" to her country. According to Benazir, the central challenge facing Pakistan was "moderation vs. extremism." She justified her dialogue with General Pervez Musharraf and expressed her hope that he "would resign from the army and restore democracy."[5]

But while she had stern words for Musharraf, Benazir feared individuals linked to the Pakistani intelligence agencies. Pakistan has three major intelligence agencies. The Intelligence Bureau (IB), the main civilian intelligence agency, focuses on domestic intelligence and reports to the prime minister; it has generally been led by a high-ranking military official. The Military Intelligence (MI) is the section of the army that specializes in intelligence and reports to the chief of army staff. The Inter-Services Intelligence (ISI) is the preeminent agency among the three. No common intelligence service, the ISI has actively intervened in political elections, organized political parties and alliances, and created and managed radical Islamic groups. It draws in the intelligence capacity of the three military service branches in addition to its own autonomous strength. Formally, the ISI communicates information to the prime minister, but in practice it reports to the chief of army staff. Benazir was particularly distrustful of ISI officers, who sympathized with religious extremists and viewed her as an enemy.

"When my flight lands in Pakistan," she wrote in the aforementioned *Washington Post* op-ed, "I know I will be greeted with joy by the people. Once I leave the airport, I pray for the best and prepare for the worst." Benazir's pessimism about her personal safety was evidenced during a private plane flight to Aspen, Colorado, where she traveled along with the US ambassador Zalmay Khalilzad and his wife, writer Cheryl Benard, shortly before Bhutto's return to Pakistan in October 2007. When a flight attendant offered Benazir some freshly baked cookies, she declined, saying she was trying to lose weight. But then she called the stewardess back and declared in an expression of black humor, "Oh what's the difference, I'll be dead in a few months anyway."[6]

Benazir and her entourage had become particularly worried about her security after official Pakistani and foreign sources communicated messages about possible militant attacks against her. The Musharraf government had told her that four suicide bomber squads would attempt to kill her. Bhutto, in turn, had written a letter to General Musharraf telling him that if militants assassinated her, it would be due to the hidden hand of close sympathizers of his regime. In the op-ed, she set October 18 as the day of her return, at which point she would assume leadership of her family's traditional party, the Pakistan People's Party (PPP), and its electoral campaign.

Musharraf was furious when Bhutto made her announcement. The general believed that her action represented "a total breach of the agreement" that Bhutto would wait until after the elections to return. Benazir apparently was equally stunned by Musharraf's irate reaction, as she perceived that no hard and fast agreement had been reached on thes issue. The inconclusive negotiations had stretched back to July 2007, when the PPP's Central Executive Committee had decided at their London meetings that Benazir would continue to head the party and that her participation in the campaign was crucial to electoral success. When Bhutto announced her decision, Musharraf's team reiterated their warnings about her security, as they continued to do after she returned.

Before her prior return to Pakistan in April 1986, Benazir had also received numerous threats and information about potential assassination plots. At that time, she had flown to Washington DC to hold meetings with Senators Ted Kennedy and Claiborne Pell, Congressman Stephen Solarz, and others. At the time, she made her decision to intensify the fight for democracy in the context of the fall of dictators Ferdinand Marcos in the Philippines and Baby Doc Duvalier in Haiti. She had received encouraging words of support, although the Reagan administration stood solidly behind dictator Zia ul-Haq. Mark Siegel, a friend, had bought Benazir a bulletproof vest. The threats in 1986 were real, but they would become a clear and present danger in the post-9/11 period.

Twenty years later, in 2007, Musharraf and his government also transmitted dramatic warnings to Benazir, but she received them with misgivings. She understood the risks that she faced. However, Bhutto felt that Musharraf was using those threats to intimidate her so that, lacking proper security, she would not return to Pakistan to campaign. Her underlying suspicion of a rigged election drove her to conduct an extensive and active campaign, with a high degree of public exposure regardless of the risk.

ON OCTOBER 18, 2007, Bhutto boarded an Emirates Airlines flight from Dubai to Karachi, landing around 1:40 p.m. at Jinnah International Airport. She had avoided flying on Pakistani International Airways because Musharraf—who ultimately controlled the state airline—could prevent the aircraft from landing. After nine years of exile, Benazir was finally returning to her home and her people. For reasons of security, a deliberate decision was made for her husband and children to remain behind. Huge crowds greeted her at the airport and along the Shahrah-e-Faisal highway. The throngs of supporters slowed down her cavalcade en route to the Muhammad Ali Jinnah mausoleum, where she was to deliver a speech.

Benazir intended to rely on her own jamming equipment to block any cell phone signals that might trigger roadside improvised explosive devices, but the Musharraf government had refused her permission to use such equipment, offering instead to provide that service for her. The arrival of bulletproof vehicles also met with obstacles, so the PPP decided to construct an armor-plated flatbed truck that put Benazir four meters off the ground to be both protected and visible to the crowds. The top of the truck had a virtually impenetrable bulletproof acrylic ledge, and the interior was insulated to ensure survival in case of a bomb attack.

She was in an upbeat mood, as were the members of the caravan and the crowds. A large group of unarmed, young volunteers holding hands—the Jaan Nisaar Benazir ("those willing to give their lives for Benazir")—formed a human shield around the vehicle.

The procession moved very slowly as night fell over Karachi. Benazir observed a curious phenomenon during the drive. As the truck approached street corners, the streetlights dimmed and then went off. A trusted aide was dispatched to the utility company KESC to lobby them to switch the lights on but was not successful. Bhutto's party colleagues and friends became agitated, as the jamming devices did not seem to be working; people in the truck were making and receiving calls on their cell phones. An attempt to contact General Musharraf's National Security Council adviser to complain about the jammers failed.

As midnight approached, and after nearly ten hours on her feet, Benazir took a rest and descended to the lower level of the truck with the former Pakistani ambassador to the United States, Abida Hussain. Then Bhutto and her political secretary, Naheed Khan, began going over the speech she would deliver at the Jinnah mausoleum. At that moment, as the truck neared the Karsaz Flyover Bridge, an explosion blew up a police van escorting Bhutto's truck, breaching the human security cordon around it. A second much more powerful explosion followed, rocking the heavy truck. The explosion perforated Benazir's eardrum, temporarily deafening her. Fire shot up around the truck. Blood and burning body parts were strewn everywhere.

Minutes earlier, a man holding up a baby dressed in PPP colors had motioned to Bhutto to take the baby, but when she asked the crowd to make way for him, he hesitated and instead tried to hand the baby over to someone in the crowd. "Don't take the baby; don't let the baby up on the truck," a loudspeaker from an escorting police car warned. By then, Bhutto had gone inside the truck. The bomb attack resulted in 149 deaths and 402 injuries. It was speculated that the baby's clothes were lined with plastic explosives.[7] Benazir, unhurt, was whisked away through back streets to Bilawal House, her family home.

After the attack, Bhutto stopped short of accusing the government but pointed the finger at individuals who she felt were abusing their positions of power.[8] She blamed factions within the military and the intelligence services of being involved in the assassination plot. Regardless, on October 21, 2007, she attempted to file a formal complaint in the form of a First Information Report (FIR) to supersede a Karachi police's FIR, which she believed to be too narrow in scope.

In her complaint, which was registered only after a protracted court process, she referred to the threat against her posed by persons she named in an October 16, 2007, letter she had sent to General Musharraf. Though Bhutto's complaint did not list these persons, Pakistani and foreign media soon reported that Bhutto's letter referred to Lieutenant General (ret.) Hamid Gul, director general of the MI under the General Zia ul-Haq dictatorship and director general of the ISI during Bhutto's first tenure as prime minister; Brigadier (ret.) Ijaz Shah, director general of the IB and former ISI official; and Chaudhry Pervaiz Elahi, Pakistan Muslim League-Quaid (PML-Q) chief minister of Punjab Province and one of Musharraf's close political allies. The Ministry of the Interior later denied any involvement by these men in the attack, while the head of the ruling PML-Q party, Chaudhry Shujaat Hussain, responded by accusing Asif Ali Zardari, Bhutto's husband, of arranging the blasts to stir up public sympathy.[9]

Benazir demanded publicly that the Federal Bureau of Investigation (FBI) or Scotland Yard be brought in to assist in the investigation of the attack. The Musharraf government immediately refused, arguing that bringing in foreign police agencies would constitute a violation of Pakistani sovereignty. Musharraf had phoned Bhutto to express his "shock and profound grief" and to assure her that a "thorough investigation would be carried out to bring the perpetrators to justice."[10] After that formal phone conversation, the two sides stopped talking to each other for several weeks.

Karachi is in Sindh Province, but the Sindh police investigation of the attack never advanced. A former high-level ISI official told our commission, however, that the ISI conducted its own investigation and, near the end of October 2007, captured and detained four suspects from a militant cell; the whereabouts of these four could not be determined by the commission during the time of our investigation.

Relations between Bhutto and Musharraf degraded further after the general, on November 3, 2007, declared emergency rule, suspended the constitution, and sacked the chief justice of Pakistan. A few days later, citing security concerns, the government placed Bhutto under house arrest. Benazir Bhutto was convinced that Musharraf was trying to intimidate her and to prevent her from campaigning for national elections. Protests, led by Bhutto's PPP, flared throughout the country, forcing him to lift the emergency rule on December 16. Despite the close call in Karachi, Bhutto resumed her electoral campaign almost immediately, requesting adequate security support from the government, which, she complained, the campaign wasn't getting. In the meantime, the former prime minister and her closest advisers continued to receive intelligence about possible bomb attacks against her in various cities.

On December 27, 2007, Bhutto was scheduled to give a speech at an electoral rally in Rawalpindi's Liaquat Bagh,[11] a park named after Prime Minister Liaquat Ali Khan, who was murdered there in 1951. Benazir feared for her life, but she felt she had to campaign for a general election—only eleven days away—that was widely believed would return her to power and steer the country to democracy.

WHAT WE KNEW about the day of Benazir Bhutto's assassination before initiating our investigation was confusing and contradictory. There were disagreements about basic facts and much controversy about the assassin or assassins, the cause of death, the former prime minister's entourage, and what the behavior of the police had been.

The campaign rally, according to witnesses, was large—in the thousands. Benazir addressed the rally from a stage, a few meters above the crowd, decorated with large portraits of her father, the founder of the PPP, Zulfikar Ali Bhutto. The crowded stage, filled with local parliamentary candidates, national party leaders, and security guards, created an atmosphere of informality and improvisation.

The police presence was relatively light, although other reports affirmed it was strong. To get in the park, people supposedly passed through metal detectors and were frisked by the police.

After Benazir concluded her speech, she boarded her bullet-proof vehicle and began to exit the park, surrounded by the Jaan Nisaar Benazir—the young male volunteers who formed her human shield. As her convoy pulled out of the park, press reports affirmed that she emerged from the vehicle's sunroof to wave to the crowd. Witnesses told a newspaper that "there was a volley of gunfire, followed almost immediately by the thunderous blast of the suicide bomb."[12]

The *New York Times* reported that Bhutto had been "shot in the neck or head, according to different accounts. . . . Seconds later a suicide bomber detonated his bomb." The news story affirmed that the attack "bore hallmarks of the Qaida-linked militants in Pakistan," although, it added, "witnesses described a sniper firing from a nearby building."[13] Some media quickly changed the story about Bhutto's cause of death, blaming shrapnel from the explosion.

A BBC News report quoted Pakistani media that suggested that the police and rangers guarding checkpoints around the exit gate of Liaquat Bagh had left their posts before Benazir's vehicle drove out of the park.[14] The BBC News also cited police sources that "confirmed reports Ms. Bhutto had been shot in the neck and chest before the gunman blew himself up."[15] Farooq Naek, a lawyer and senior official of the PPP, gave a slightly different version to Agence France Presse: "Two bullets hit her, one in the abdomen and one in the head."[16]

DawnNews TV, a respected Pakistani news organization with a TV channel and a major print and electronic daily newspaper in English, aired blurry images of an armed assassin wearing sunglasses opening fire at Bhutto "with remarkable aplomb," one or two meters away from the vehicle with no one obstructing him or the vehicle. A "professional sharpshooter" was the way many characterized the lone assassin. However, other witnesses claimed there were two attackers: a gunman and a suicide bomber.

Dawn newspaper asserted, based on images telecast by DawnNews TV, that it was "abundantly clear that there was no security cordon around Ms. Bhutto's vehicle . . . giving lie to the government claim that she had received VIP security."[17] PPP activist Zamurd Khan was quoted by the *New York Times* as saying that Benazir had been shot in the head from gunfire that originated from behind her vehicle "in a building nearby."[18]

The *Telegraph* indicated, quoting a leader of the PPP, that "two shots hit Ms. Bhutto in the neck and shoulder." It further reported that "a doctor on the team that attended her said the main cause of death was a bullet that entered the back of her neck and damaged her spinal cord before exiting the side of her head. Another bullet pierced the back of her shoulder and came through her chest."[19]

A report by RTT News[20] announced that the perpetrator of the assassination had been identified. It also cited PPP activists who singled out Khalid Shahenshah, one of Benazir's security guards who had subsequently gone underground and who had been caught on TV footage making suspicious signals while standing on the dais next to Bhutto, prior to the exit from the rally where she was murdered. Shahenshah was positioned to Bhutto's left during her speech, and he continually glanced to his left and crouched down several times as if, according to some, to get out of the line of fire, while appearing to run his fingers across his throat—a universal gesture for death. The same RTT report mentioned that Bhutto had hired Shahenshah on the recommendation of security adviser Rehman Malik, minister of the interior at the time of the launching of the UN Commission of Inquiry.

As will be discussed later, the commission heard numerous conflicting accounts of Benazir's trip to the hospital. At Rawalpindi General Hospital, doctors tried for thirty-five minutes to resuscitate the former prime minister without success. Dr. Abbas Hayat declared to the press that Bhutto had wounds to her head as well as shrapnel injuries. Dr. Muhammad Mussadiq Khan, a top surgeon who attended Bhutto at the hospital, said that she was "clinically dead" on arrival. No autopsy was performed, DawnNews TV reported, because the police did not request one. The government replied that Bhutto's husband, Asif Ali Zardari, had waived the autopsy.

AFTER THE ATTACK, the scene of the blast was quickly washed with a high-pressure hose by the local fire company. A day later, Brigadier Javed Cheema of the Interior Ministry gave a press conference where he informed the media that Bhutto had died of a skull fracture caused by a lever attached to the sunroof of her bulletproof vehicle. He further announced that intercepted communications permitted the government to state that Baitullah Mehsud, a tribal leader in northwestern Pakistan, had ordered the assassination with support from Al-Qaida's terrorist network.

The CIA came to the same conclusion according to declarations made by the agency's director, Michael V. Hayden. Some George W. Bush administration officials outside the CIA who dealt with Pakistani matters were less confident, with one, according to the *Washington Post*, qualifying Hayden's assertion as merely "a very good assumption."[21]

The controversy surrounding Bhutto's death forced the Musharraf government to agree to a narrow probe by Scotland Yard to "support and assist" the Pakistani authorities in establishing the "precise cause" of Bhutto's death.

The PPP leaders strongly disagreed with the notion that Benazir had died from an accidental wound caused by hitting her head against the lever of the sunroof of the vehicle. Sherry Rehman, spokeswoman for the Pakistan People's Party, who was with Bhutto in the hospital declared, "She died from a bullet injury. This was and is our position."[22] Senator Safdar Abbasi, a medical doctor and longtime friend of Benazir, who was actually in the vehicle with her at the time of the fatal attack reasoned that "the way she died—an instant death—suggests very sharp sniper fire, a typical intelligence operation."[23] His wife, Naheed Khan, who was also a passenger in Bhutto's vehicle on December 27, agreed: "There were bullets coming from different directions. . . . There are lots of high buildings overlooking the area. . . . This was a typical intelligence operation."[24]

The PPP demanded a United Nations investigation of the assassination. In early January 2008, widower and now PPP leader, Asif Ali Zardari, wrote in the *Washington Post*, "I call on the United Nations to commence a thorough investigation on the circumstances, facts and cover-up of my wife's murder, modeled on the investigation into the assassination of former Lebanese Prime Minister Rafiq-al-Hariri."[25] When Zardari became president of Pakistan on September 6, 2008, the call became not merely a popular notion but an official request from a United Nations member state to the secretary-general of the organization. Five months later, Ban Ki-moon's office called me in Chile and the investigation began.

Pakistani prime minister Liaquat Ali Khan meets US president Harry S. Truman during a visit to the United States in May 1950. Prime Minister Khan was assassinated in 1951 at Company Bagh, later renamed Liaquat Bagh, the same location where Benazir Bhutto was killed in 2007.

2

An Early History of Instability

On October 16, 1951, around 4:00 p.m., Pakistan's first prime minister, Liaquat Ali Khan, arrived at Company Bagh (East India Company Gardens) in Rawalpindi for a political rally. A crowd of about one hundred thousand people had assembled to listen to a public speech by the prime minister in a meeting organized by the Pakistan Muslim League. Prime Minister Ali Khan was in good spirits. He had told his wife he was going to make the speech of his life.[1]

The prime minister had instructed his assistants that only he would address the crowd and that he'd be alone on the dais, sitting on the sole available chair. There would be no protective canopy above the platform so that people would have a full view of their leader.

The meeting began at 4:10 p.m. with the recitation of the Holy Quran, followed by brief welcoming introductions by the president of the municipal committee and by the president of the city Muslim League, who invited the prime minister to address the multitude.

Prime Minister Ali Khan walked to the microphone and had

barely said, "Baradran-i-millat" (Dear brothers) when two shots from a 9mm pistol rang in the air. The prime minister, hit by a bullet, staggered and fell on his back, mortally wounded. A few seconds later, another shot rang out, followed by silence and surprise first, and then by cries and weeping from the crowd as they realized their leader had been hit.

The assailant who had fired on the prime minister was quickly seized and beaten by people in the crowd. The killer was a twenty-nine-year-old Afghan by the name of Said Akbar, the son of a tribal leader of Khost, Afghanistan. Akbar was residing in Abbottabad—the same town that, decades later, would become famous as the final hideout of Osama bin Laden.

An unconscious prime minister was rushed to the Combined Military Hospital in Rawalpindi, where all efforts to save him failed. He succumbed to his wounds at 4:50 p.m.

Even though the crowd had overpowered and disarmed the assassin, a police subinspector shot the man, killing him instantly. Despite having given his subordinate the order to shoot the assailant, Police Superintendent Khan Najaf Khan rushed from thirteen yards away to fire point-blank at Akbar five times.

The park where Prime Minister Ali Khan was assassinated became known as Liaquat Bagh—the same place where Prime Minister Benazir Bhutto would be murdered almost sixty years later. One of the emergency doctors who attended Prime Minister Ali Khan was the father of Dr. Mussadiq Khan, one of the doctors who, fifty-six years later, tried to revive Benazir Bhutto.[2]

The elimination of the assassin Said Akbar by the police only fueled conspiracy theories that are still around today. Akbar had significant amounts of money at his home in Abbottabad and on his person, which suggested he might have been a hired assassin. Akbar and his brother had participated in a failed uprising against the Afghan king's government in the mid-

1940s and had ended up receiving protection and a pension from Great Britain. In January 1954, the Pakistani government announced that it intended to request an American FBI investigation into the assassination of Prime Minister Liaquat, but the request never materialized. Instead, a retired Scotland Yard detective was hired and produced a report concluding that the murder had been the work of a lone fanatic. Earlier, a promising Pakistani police investigation was frustrated when the inspector responsible for it, Nawbazada Mirza Aitizazuddin, died in a plane crash on August 26, 1952.[3] An article written in 2010 by a Pakistani scholar argues that the Afghan was not really the assassin, as an inquiry commission appointed by the government concluded, but that he was a scapegoat and that the prime minister had been killed as part of an obscure and cold-blooded political plot.[4]

SINCE THE VERY birth of Pakistan, following independence from Britain and the partition of India in August 1947, the country has experienced a history marked by violence, military rule, and political corruption. Just months after the partition, the country suffered the untimely natural death in 1948 of Muhammad Ali Jinnah, the father of the nation and first governor-general. Jinnah had agitated for the twin goals of independence from British rule and the creation of an independent state for India's Muslims, but despite this religious preference, he had intended to build a secular, democratic state.[5] His death and the country's first war with India, over the disputed territories of Kashmir, sidelined efforts to construct a stable political system and marked the beginning of a cycle of violence, wars, and enmity that has endured until today.

Moreover, ethnic nationalism would erode the idea of Pakistan as a multiethnic state with equal rights for all. Despite the stated goal of ethnic equality, there has always been a perception of Punjabi dominance. At different moments, Baloch nationalists, Pashtun nationalists, Bengalis in East Pakistan, Sindhis, and Muhajirs have questioned that order and clashed with the central government and each other, at times seeking greater autonomy through uprisings.

After Jinnah's death, the country experienced the loss of another leader with the assassination of Liaquat Ali Khan. Pakistan's first few years as an independent nation were marked with instability.

During the 1950s, Pakistan had seven different prime ministers, each unsuccessfully attempting to complete the five-year terms established by law. Amid growing chaos in 1958, General Ayub Khan seized power from President Iskander Mirza in a bloodless coup d'état. Twenty days earlier, Mirza had instituted martial law and abrogated the 1956 constitution. From 1958 on, the military's entrenchment in Pakistani politics would become the norm.

Self-appointed field marshal Ayub Khan, the only five-star general in Pakistan's military history, promised to lift martial law and called on several politicians to join the new government. Benazir's father, Zulfikar Ali Bhutto, a young highly educated and brilliant politician, was one of those approached by the military. Despite his reservations about serving a military regime, he joined as minister of fuel, power, and natural resources.

Pakistan, like all nations at the time, was caught up in the polarization of the Cold War. The country was becoming a bastion for the United States in the growing East-West conflict, allowing a large CIA office to be set up in Karachi, permitting U-2 spy planes to fly over the Soviet Union from an air base near Peshawar, and joining SEATO—the Southeast Asian counterpart of NATO—after signing a Mutual Defense Assistance Agreement with the United States in May 1954. India and other countries from the region refused to become part of SEATO. The Central Treaty Organization (CENTO) followed in 1955 as an attempt to secure US interests in the Middle East; again, Pakistan joined.

Not sharing the pro-US sentiment of his colleagues, Bhutto negotiated an important oil agreement with the Soviet Union and began to build an independent power base within the Ayub government, favoring Third World and nonaligned policies. In 1963 he was named foreign minister and began to openly disagree with General Ayub's continuing alliance with Washington. Ayub did not care much about foreign policy, except to safeguard Pakistan's alliance with the United States to ensure that American money would continue to flow to the military. Once Bhutto took the helm of Pakistan's foreign policy, the US money dried up.

Relations between Pakistan and China deteriorated under General Ayub, as SEATO was an evident American instrument aimed at China. Bhutto, however, engineered a rapprochement with China. The two countries signed a historic border agreement, resumed official trade relations, and, in 1964, Beijing gave Pakistan an interest-free loan of $60 million to compensate for the loss of US aid.

The United States withheld aid to Pakistan while, at the same time, increasing it to Pakistan's rival, India. In 1965 General Ayub was uninvited to visit Washington after Zulfikar Ali Bhutto opposed the expanding American war in Vietnam.

But the catalyst for the breakup between Bhutto and Ayub came as a result of the 1965 war with India over Jammu and Kashmir. Surprisingly, the White House cut off military aid to both sides, disappointing Pakistan, which assumed the United States would be on the side of its SEATO and CENTO ally.

India, by contrast, was supported by the Soviet Union. Only China came out in support of Pakistan, declaring India the aggressor in the war and issuing an ultimatum to India to withdraw its military deployment along the China-Sikkim border.

The 1965 India-Pakistan war ended when both accepted a UN Security Council resolution to cease all hostilities. At the Soviet Union's behest, General Ayub and Indian leaders met in Tashkent, where the Tashkent Agreement was signed detailing the withdrawal of troops, the repatriation of POWs, and the restoration of the cease-fire line. Bhutto opposed the Tashkent Agreement, resigned as foreign minister, and left the Ayub government. Bhutto's popularity grew considerably following his resignation.

Meanwhile, discontent flourished in Pakistan as Mahbub ul-Haq—a distinguished Pakistani economist who, along with Amartya Sen, conceived the United Nations Development Programme's "human development" approach to measure development beyond economic growth—denounced the increasing concentration of wealth and growing disparities in his own country among individuals and regions, including East and West Pakistan.

The Ayub regime began to harass the Bhutto family businesses as Zulfikar became a more strident public critic of the regime. Bhutto then decided to create his own political party, and on November 30, 1967, despite an Ayub regime ban on public meetings, delegates met in the garden of a private house to found Bhutto's Pakistan People's Party. The PPP had a populist message summed up in the slogan, "Roti, kapra, aur makam" (Bread, clothing, and shelter).

As the Ayub regime progressively lost ground, the PPP grew into the most powerful party in West Pakistan, while the Awami League, under the direction of Sheikh Mujibur Rahman, surged as the predominant force in East Pakistan.

The Awami League put forward a six-point program in 1966, in which it demanded significant degrees of autonomy for East Pakistan, with the federal government only limited to the areas of defense and foreign policy. Rahman also demanded a complete reform of the political system and the end of Ayub's regime. Ayub rejected the six-point program and, in 1968, had Mujibur Rahman arrested.

Against a backdrop of rising instability and Ayub's heart ailment, on March 26, 1969, General Agha Mohammad Yahya Khan, the army's commander in chief, proclaimed martial law, abrogated the 1962 constitution, assumed the presidency of Pakistan, surrounding himself with a team of military advisers, and promised elections for the following year. Ayub left quietly.

Elections were held in December 1970, with twenty-three parties disputing 291 seats in the National Assembly. As expected, the Awami League won handily in East Pakistan, and Bhutto's PPP won the majority of seats in West Pakistan (split into four provinces instead of "One Unit," as was the case until then). The military had underestimated the force of Bhutto's populist platform and overestimated the support for the religious and conservative parties. In a memoir, former Pakistani ambassador Jamsheed Marker reveals that the then US national security adviser Henry Kissinger told him, "Everywhere else in the world elections help to solve problems; in Pakistan they seem to create them."[6]

Negotiations toward an agreement to share power between the Awami League and the PPP were vetoed by the army in March 1971, and riots broke out in East Pakistan, which, at the time, made up 56 percent of Pakistan's population.

The military violently repressed the demonstrations in East Pakistan. Talks between General Yahya Khan, Bhutto, and

Mujibur failed, and the army proceeded to ban the Awami League, arrest Mujibur, and forbid political activities in all of Pakistan. The country plunged into civil war, and the army massacred thousands of East Pakistani rebels. Within a few months, millions of Bengalis became refugees, and many of them flowed from East Pakistan to India seeking safe haven.

By the second half of 1971, India began to train and equip a Bengali liberation army. Soon after, General Yahya Khan announced an all-out war; a provisional government of Bangladesh was formed. Following Pakistani air strikes across the cease-fire line in Kashmir into northern India in early December 1971, the New Delhi government launched massive attacks into East Pakistan, controlling the territory within a few days and recognizing the provisional government of Bangladesh.

On December 16, Pakistani military forces surrendered, and a cease-fire was put in place. General Yahya Khan had no option but to resign; he handed the presidency over to Zulfikar Ali Bhutto, who had just returned to Islamabad from the UN Security Council in New York, where he had been sent to do the impossible: salvage the Pakistani position.

BHUTTO BECAME PAKISTAN'S president and civilian administrator of martial law. He quickly strengthened relations with China and was able to get from the Chinese a write-off of significant loans and the cost of new military hardware. Around that time, he initiated Pakistan's nuclear program, which was accelerated when, in May 1974, India tested a nuclear bomb. In parallel, Bhutto negotiated with Indira Gandhi the Simla Agreement that normalized, to a great extent, bilateral relations between the two countries. The Simla Agreement was considered a big success for Bhutto, who had traveled to the negotiations in northern India accompanied by his young daughter

Benazir, who became a privileged observer of the negotiations. In 1972, Bhutto also rescinded martial law and tasked the National Assembly with drafting a new constitution.

Among Bhutto's major accomplishments was the 1973 constitution, approved by consensus in August of that year. Under the new constitution, Zulfikar assumed the post of prime minister, relinquishing the presidency, which was largely ceremonial by then. The 1973 constitution defined Pakistan as a federal Islamic republic with a parliamentary government. Meanwhile, the PPP mobilized millions of people in favor of secularism and democracy and against mullahs and the military.

The Pakistan Muslim League, once the party of the moderate Jinnah, had become the party of the military, which, in the new constitution, saw its powers curtailed at the hands of the federal government. Bhutto masterminded domestic industrialization, land reform, and infrastructure works and pursued an activist foreign policy, which had as its highlight the holding of the Islamic Summit of the Organization of the Islamic Conference (OIC) in Lahore in 1974.

Controlling the levers of power, Bhutto amended the 1973 constitution to allow the federal government to ban political parties and curb the autonomy of the courts. Fearful of army plots against him, Bhutto had a group of officers arrested in April 1973. He also removed General Gul Hassan, the army commander in chief, and Air Marshal Rahim Khan, the air force chief, accusing them of "Bonapartism" and sending them off in golden exile as ambassadors to Vienna and Madrid, respectively.

Bhutto had already given in to the pressures of the small religious parties in the 1973 constitution by declaring that Pakistan was an "Islamic state" in which only a Muslim could become its president or prime minister, and establishing the Council of

Islamic Ideology, charged with the Islamization of laws. Years later, when embattled and needing political support, he made further concessions to religious parties by banning alcohol, driving the country's gambling and entertainment sector underground, supporting a parliamentary motion to declare the Ahmadis as non-Muslims, and declaring Fridays the day of prayers, a public holiday.

In 1976, Zulfikar Ali Bhutto named General Zia ul-Haq as army commander in chief, going over the heads of five senior generals. Zia was perceived as obedient, lacking in political aspirations, and a religious, unsophisticated individual. He was also the first army commander who was not from the elite ranks of the military academy.

In the run-up to the national parliamentary elections, the country was rocked by disorder, boycotts, and strikes organized by an opposition coalition and, according to Bhutto, supposedly funded by the United States. In July 1977, General ul-Haq overthrew Zulfikar Ali Bhutto, declared martial law, and appointed himself chief martial law administrator. Prime Minister Bhutto was arrested.

Bhutto had introduced important social and economic changes, campaigned against the military-religious alliance that had ruled Pakistan for years, and turned Pakistan into a nuclear country—a development not welcomed by the United States and other powers. But toward the end of his administration, Zulfikar had turned into an autocratic ruler, rigged parliamentary elections, and given in to Islamists in his attempt to hold on to power.

Zulfikar Ali Bhutto was released and rearrested several times until the Zia dictatorship accused him of conspiracy to murder a political opponent, Ahmed Raza Kasuri. A maverick member of the PPP, Kasuri had been shot at three years earlier in an incident in which his father died. An initial inquiry by the High Court had cleared Prime Minister Bhutto of any connection to the crime. After being denied a slot in the PPP ticket to Parliament, Kasuri decided to cooperate with the military by once again filing charges against Bhutto.

Despite a vigorous international campaign and appeals by several heads of state to save Bhutto's life after a death sentence was handed down by the Supreme Court, the former prime minister was executed on April 4, 1979. He died in the central jail of Rawalpindi, the garrison city where Pakistan's first prime minister, Liaquat Ali Khan, had been assassinated and the same city where Zulfikar Ali Bhutto's daughter, Benazir, was to be murdered.

Benazir Bhutto's family in July 1978. From left to right are Benazir's mother, Begum Nusrat Bhutto; brother Shahnawaz Bhutto; father and former prime minister, Zulfikar Ali Bhutto; and Benazir next to her father. Brother Mir Murtaza Bhutto is seated at bottom left and sister Sanam Bhutto at bottom right. Sanam, who kept a low profile in active politics, is the sole surviving member of the family today.

3

Violence in the Family and in the Nation

AT THE TIME of her father's death, Benazir Bhutto had no intention of becoming a politician, because she had seen firsthand the strains of life in politics. Instead, she aspired to become a diplomat in Pakistan's Foreign Service. In her late teens, Benazir enjoyed accompanying her father to summits and state visits, like the one to the United States in 1973 when she was seated next to Henry Kissinger at a White House dinner or, in February 1974, when the twenty-year-old flew home to join her father and the rest of the family at the Islamic Summit that the prime minister had convened in Lahore.

Between 1969 and 1973, Benazir attended Radcliffe College at Harvard, where she obtained a bachelor's degree, majoring in government. College offered new experiences for the young woman accustomed to a life of privilege. This was the first time she walked to classes, since in Pakistan a chauffeur always drove her around and picked her up. Benazir wrote that in the United States, at Radcliffe, she "experienced democracy for the first time" and that there she had spent "four of the happiest years of [her] life."[1]

Bhutto urged his daughter to leave the United States, so as not to put down roots, to attend Oxford University. She arrived at Oxford in the autumn of 1973 to undertake graduate-level courses in philosophy, politics, and law; from there, Benazir traveled to Pakistan regularly. "I feel a strange sensation in imagining you walking on the footprints I left behind at Oxford twenty-two years ago," wrote Prime Minister Bhutto affectionately to his daughter as she entered Oxford.[2] Zulfikar Ali Bhutto had encouraged his daughter to study the lives of legendary female leaders like Joan of Arc and Indira Gandhi. At Oxford, Benazir soon demonstrated her talents as a leader by becoming the first Asian woman to head the prestigious Oxford Union debating society. During her time at Oxford, Benazir also reconnected with her younger brother Mir Murtaza, who began his first year there in 1976.

Benazir was twenty-four years old when she returned to Pakistan in 1977, after completing her studies at Oxford. She was excited about her homecoming. Her father had arranged for her to work at the prime minister's office during the summer and at the Inter-Provincial Council of Common Interests. In September Benazir would be part of the Pakistani delegation to the United Nations General Assembly debates, and she would return to Pakistan in November to take her foreign ministry exams in December. But when she returned to her country in June of that year, it was to witness the downfall of her father and to face house arrest and imprisonment under the Zia dictatorship.

Zulfikar Ali Bhutto's death, by order of the Zia-controlled judiciary, was a defining moment for Benazir. She decided to become a politician in order to take on the military dictator and to preserve her father's legacy. She inherited the mantle of leadership of her father's PPP, although Zulfikar's wife, Begum

Nusrat Bhutto, had been named acting chairperson. Benazir's youngest brothers, Mir Murtaza and Shahnawaz, went into exile to attempt to organize a resistance against the Zia dictatorship. In Pakistan, Nusrat and Benazir spent time in jail, while the Zia regime arrested and tortured thousands of opposition activists, banned politics, censored the media, and introduced new Islamic laws that victimized non-Muslim minorities and women.

The Zia dictatorship engaged in a tight alliance with the United States to carry out joint actions against the recent Soviet occupation of Afghanistan. More importantly, Zia, a highly religious man, deepened Sunni-led Islamization of Pakistan and of the army. In his first public statement following the coup in July 1977, Zia declared, "Pakistan, which was created in the name of Islam, will continue to survive only if it sticks to Islam." He viewed the Islamic system as "an essential prerequisite for the country."[3] Government offices were instructed to allow both time and space for daily prayers, which heads of departments were expected to lead. The dress code of the bureaucracy changed from ties and three-piece suits to achkans, shalwars, and waistcoats. Public displays of piety began to be considered good form. The rituals changed in army officers' messes, with the disappearance of formal dinner nights at which port wine traditionally concluded the evenings' meals. During the holy month of Ramadan, restaurants and food concessions were ordered to close from sunrise to sundown. Smoking cigarettes, drinking water, or eating in public during Ramadan became punishable by arrest. Zia's Shariat courts issued the Hudood Ordinances under which, for example, four Muslim men were required as witnesses to prove a woman's charge of rape. Without such evidence, a woman claiming she had been raped could be charged with adultery. Despite professional women's protests, in 1984 the Law of Evidence was passed, under which a woman's testimony was made worth only half that of a man's testimony.

Maulana Maudoodi, the leader of the extremist religious party Jamaat-e-Islami, became the spiritual father of the dictator and a major supporter in Zia's efforts to raise funds for the Afghan mujahideen. Allied with the Reagan administration, Zia increased the size of the ISI agency to organize and support the mujahideen in their battle against the Soviets. The ISI channeled about $8 billion from the US government to the Afghan fighters and trained the Taliban troops.

General Zia made the works of Maulana Maudoodi compulsory reading in the armed forces. Maudoodi, who had strong ties with the Saudi clergy, considered Ali Jinnah, the founder of Pakistan, a "nonbeliever" and also declared Zulfikar Ali Bhutto and Benazir to be nonbelievers. Maudoodi, together with the ISI and the army, became key pillars of Zia's dictatorship.

Deobandi madrassas flourished under Zia ul-Haq. The Deobandi movement was rooted in a school of thought originating from the Dar ul-Ulum madrassa in 1867 in Deoband, India, the members of which were as conservative as the Wahhabis in Saudi Arabia. The power of the civil courts declined as Sharia courts and military tribunals gained ground, supported by Zia. He created the International Islamic University in Islamabad to gather leading Wahhabis and the Muslim Brotherhood. In December 1984, Zia held a referendum on Islamization, with voters having to choose between a "yes" vote in favor of Islamic laws and General Zia ul-Haq staying in power or a "no" vote. Zia got 98 percent approval in his referendum.

In 1981, nine political parties, including some that had opposed Zulfikar Ali Bhutto, united into the Movement for the Restoration of Democracy (MRD), demanding the holding of "free, fair, and impartial elections." When the Zia regime refused, the MRD took its opposition to the streets. Benazir, just twenty-eight at the time, would become the leader of the movement.

The Zia regime repeatedly arrested Benazir or kept her under house arrest for nearly six years. The press was banned from printing the Bhutto name. Benazir was severely affected by her father's death, and in prison she suffered ear infections and other ailments. In 1984, thanks to international pressure on her behalf, she was released from jail for medical treatment and allowed to travel to London; from there, she began to lobby throughout Europe and the United States for Pakistani democracy.

With her mother Nusrat's support, and while her two younger brothers were in exile trying to mount a movement of armed resistance to the dictatorship, Benazir formally supplanted Nusrat and assumed the title of chairperson of her father's party, which she already controlled. In 1986 she decided to return to Pakistan. On April 10, 1986, she arrived in Lahore to a welcome by hundreds of thousands of Pakistanis. Thereafter, Benazir became the face of Zia ul-Haq's opposition.

In May 1988, General Zia dismissed his handpicked prime minister Muhammed Khan Junejo, dissolved Parliament, and called for elections. A few weeks later, in June, Zia announced that Sharia law was now the supreme law of the land. He also announced that the elections would be held on a political partyless basis and that there would be no party symbols on the ballots. Benazir went to the Supreme Court to challenge Zia's election rules, hoping for free and fair elections.

On the morning of August 17, 1988, General Zia ul-Haq, accompanied by five other generals, the US ambassador to Pakistan, Arnold Raphel, and the American military attaché, flew to Bahawalpur, about 330 miles south of Islamabad; they then headed by helicopter to a test site to watch a demonstration of an American-made battle tank, which the Pentagon was pressing Pakistan to purchase. With the tests over, Zia and his entourage returned to Bahawalpur for lunch. After the meal, Zia excused himself to say his prayers, and soon after, the party boarded the presidential plane, a Lockheed C-130, to fly back to Islamabad.

The C-130 took off from Bahawalpur on schedule at 3:46 p.m. Soon after takeoff, the presidential plane failed to respond to the control tower. Witnesses saw the aircraft plunging and exploding into a ball of fire as it hit the ground at 3:51 p.m. The mystery surrounding the plane crash has never dissipated.

A joint Pakistani-US investigation of the crash never came to a conclusion. A separate Pakistani inquiry yielded a 365-page secret report—of which only a 27-page summary was released—ruling out mechanical failure as causing the crash and concluding that it had been the result of an act of sabotage. Although no firm evidence of an explosion in the aircraft was discovered, the Pakistani report asserted that chemicals that could be used in small explosives were found in mango seeds or peels on board and on a piece of rope in the aircraft.[4] General Mahmud Ali Durrani, the officer in charge of the tank tests, had loaded two boxes of local mangoes on the plane. He had ordered the mangoes to be thoroughly checked, although more had been loaded at the Bahawalpur Airport over which he claimed he had no control. The report added that the "use of a chemical agent to incapacitate the pilots, and thus perpetrate the accident, [remained] a distinct probability."[5] However, no autopsies were performed on the crew to ascertain if they had been poisoned by gas.

Many theories emerged about the crash. Hamid Gul, the director of the ISI at the time, told the *Times* that Zia ul-Haq had been killed in a conspiracy involving "a foreign power."[6] The suggestion was that the CIA had carried out the assassination, even though high American officials were among the victims. Another version blamed the KGB acting in retaliation against Zia for his strong support of the Afghan mujahideen insurgency against the Soviets.

The US Congress held a number of hearings about the crash, but no official report was ever made public. The FBI was kept away from the case for a year, under orders from the Pentagon, and its eventual investigation came too late to examine critical evidence. Although the US Air Force concluded that the crash had been caused by a mechanical problem common to the C-130 aircraft, John Gunther Dean, then US ambassador to India, pointed the finger at the Mossad, the Israeli intelligence agency. He believed they orchestrated Zia's assassination in retaliation for Pakistan's having developed nuclear weapons to counteract India but eventually use against Israel, and to disrupt the Pakistani-American alliance.[7]

Former deputy director of the CIA Vernon Walters wrote in his autobiographical book, *The Mighty and the Meek*, that the plane crash that killed Zia "may or may not have been caused by sabotage."[8] Another theory, with little supporting evidence, pointed to some dissatisfied army generals and even to the pilot of the C-130 plane, who, supposedly, had confided to an associate that he hated Zia for his repression of the Shia religious leaders. Zia ul-Haq's son Ijaz ul-Haq, in an interview with *New York Times* reporter Barbara Crossette a year after the crash, said that he was "101 percent sure" that the armed resistance group of Mir Murtaza Bhutto had been responsible for blowing up the plane.[9]

Despite the enduring mystery, Zia's death reopened the window to democracy in Pakistan. Ghulam Ishaq Khan, president of the Senate, assumed the role of acting president and, knowing where power lay, immediately asked the new head of the army, General Mirza Aslam Beg, what he wanted to do with the country. General Beg opted for democratic elections in the fall of 1988. Benazir decided to compete for a seat in Parliament.

Elections were held in November 1988, and Lieutenant General Hamid Gul, the director general of the ISI, played an active role in vote rigging and manipulation. Great swaths of ISI money helped create a right-wing coalition of nine Islamic parties and the Muslim League—the Islamic Democratic Alliance. Despite the interference of the ISI, Benazir and the PPP emerged triumphant, beating Zia's protégé, Nawaz Sharif.

BEFORE THE ELECTIONS, in December 1987, Benazir had married Asif Ali Zardari in Karachi. Prior to that, being in her thirties and single, she decided that it wasn't proper to aspire to become prime minister as an unmarried woman. The Pakistani public was barely ready for a modern, highly educated female leader, let alone a single woman. Benazir feared that few men would accept her as a serious political figure in an Islamic society. Zardari, an avid polo player who had his own squad, a lover of living the high life (young Zardari reportedly had set up a disco in his house), and a member of the land-owning Zardari tribe from Sindh Province, did not have that problem, though he was clearly her inferior. Bhutto's mother and an aunt arranged the marriage, which Benazir justified by comparing it to computer dating.[10] She recognized that her friends in the West would find it difficult to understand the peculiar cultural and political circumstances that had led her to an arranged marriage.[11]

Benazir had grown progressively apart from her two brothers, Mir Murtaza and Shahnawaz, who disagreed with her realpolitik approach to Pakistani public life and Zardari's growing political influence. Mir had urged his father to resist the Zia coup, but Zulfikar had responded that one must never resist a military coup. On their father's instructions, Mir and Shahnawaz reluctantly left for England and Switzerland, respectively. Benazir stayed behind in Pakistan to help her father with his defense and to maintain popular support in the streets. Schooled in English, Benazir had to be tutored in Urdu so she could speak on her jailed father's behalf. Benazir toured the provinces coached by her father.

Mir and Shahnawaz left their studies and dedicated themselves full-time to the cause of gathering international support for their imprisoned father. Playing the role of the responsible eldest sibling, Benazir wrote to Mir to pass on instructions from her father to avoid a lavish lifestyle abroad and to refuse interviews with Indian and Israeli papers, for they could be politically misconstrued in Pakistan. After their father's death, Mir and Shahnawaz went into exile to organize an armed resistance against the dictator, first from neighboring Afghanistan and later from Syria.

In the summer of 1985, the Bhuttos decided to hold a family reunion in Nice, France. Shahnawaz, the youngest of Benazir's brothers, had decided to live in the open, abandoning Syria and ceasing to organize armed resistance and violence against Zia's dictatorship.

Nusrat, Benazir's mother, traveled from Geneva, Mir Murtaza from Damascus, and Benazir and sister Sanam from London. The extended family, including children, spent happy days at the beach practicing sports, organizing barbecues, and dining out.

Benazir recalled in her autobiography that Shahnawaz seemed happy, except for the fact that he intended to divorce his wife, Rehana, from whom he had separated twice already, reconciling each time because of their daughter.[12] Shahnawaz, whom the family called "Shah," was concerned about Benazir's security and took her shopping for a bulletproof vest. Shahnawaz was also considered a target of the Zia dictatorship, particularly because he was the military leader of the two brothers, while Mir was the politician. Mir told his sister that both brothers carried vials of poison wherever they went in case they were caught by Zia agents—thus opting for death instead of prison.

On the morning of July 18, Mir received a phone call from Shah's wife, who asked him to urgently come and see his brother. "Something is wrong" with Shahnawaz, Rehana declared. Upon entering Shah's apartment, they found him lying face down on the living room floor. He was dead. Mir told the police who arrived on the scene that he suspected that his brother had been poisoned, adding that Shah had already survived four attempts on his life; but no immediate proof could be found to support that assertion. Subsequent police investigation did reveal, however, that there was a strong poison in his system.

Theories about his death spread quickly. Some said that he had committed suicide, a hypothesis denied by the closest relatives and the circumstances of the Bhutto family get-together. Others asserted that Shahnawaz had been murdered over arguments about family assets stashed away in Switzerland. The Zia-controlled press reported that Shah had been a suicidal gambler. The police investigated Rehana because nine hours had passed before the family and police had been summoned to the scene and because the couple had a stormy relationship. Benazir and Mir Murtaza filed a murder case against unknown persons. The police arrested Rehana under the charge of not having aided her dying husband, but they eventually released her and allowed her to leave France.

Benazir personally accompanied Shah's body to Pakistan on August 21, 1985, after the Zia regime reluctantly agreed to allow his burial in Larkana. She was arrested five days later in Karachi and remained under house arrest—despite expressions of "dismay" by the Reagan administration—until November 3 when she was allowed to leave for France to give her deposition on the death case of her brother.

The theory that General Zia had ordered the hit on Shahnawaz's life gained ground with time. But the case was never solved, and no responsible party was ever identified.[13]

ON DECEMBER 2, 1988, at the age of thirty-five, Bhutto was sworn in as the democratically elected prime minister, the youngest person and first woman in history ever elected to head an Islamic state. Bhutto's party had won the largest number of seats in the National Assembly but had not secured a clear majority. She had defeated Nawaz Sharif, the ISI-backed candidate who, following his supporters' recommendation, secured the post of chief minister of Punjab Province instead of holding a seat in the National Assembly. Hamid Gul, the ISI director general, and General Asad Durrani, ex–ISI chief and, at the time, MI director, prided themselves on Nawaz Sharif's loyalty to the legacy of Zia ul-Haq who had returned to Sharif the family-owned steel mill business, nationalized by Zulfikar Ali Bhutto. They believed that although he had been defeated on this occasion, Sharif could exercise power in Punjab, beyond Benazir's reach. Nawaz supporters affirmed that Benazir would functionally be the prime minister of the capital only—not in the rest of the country.

The army initially refused to allow Bhutto to assume her duties as prime minister, but Washington stepped in to broker a deal: Benazir would leave foreign policy and the nuclear program in the hands of the army and she would agree not to interfere in the military or defense sector budget and promotions. Also, several Zia supporters would continue in government functions.

Bhutto introduced various modernization reforms. She lifted bans affecting labor unions and student associations, ordered the release of political prisoners, removed constraints on the functioning of nongovernmental organizations, favored uncensored media reporting, and sought to improve ties with India. Benazir reversed some policies introduced by her father, including returning Pakistan to the British Commonwealth and privatizing some industries that her father had nationalized or placed in the public sector. Accused of favoring Westernization, the new prime minister decided to cover her head with a white *dupatta*, which her father had once recommended she wear when visiting the conservative tribal areas. She was the first woman in the Bhutto family to hide her hair, apparently a political move to keep the support of Islamic groups and leaders.

Five months after she became prime minister, she dismissed General Hamid Gul from his position as director general of the ISI, which controlled the Pakistani participation in the ongoing Afghan war, because she had learned that Gul was conspiring with the opposition to oust her from power. Hamid Gul and the army were so powerful that Benazir could not retire the general but only transfer him to another important post. She named a retired general as head of the ISI, a move that bothered army commander General Beg. Consequently, he isolated the ISI and instructed the MI to fill the void.

Osama bin Laden appeared in the Pakistani political landscape in late October 1989 when, according to Benazir Bhutto, he provided $10 million to fund a no-confidence vote in Parliament against the prime minister. The objective was to buy out supporters of Bhutto in the National Assembly so as to overthrow her government and install, with the help of ISI officers, a theocratic regime in Pakistan.[14] Benazir phoned US president George H. W. Bush to let him know that Pakistani military hardliners who had supported the mujahideen now were attempting to bring down her government with the help of foreign money. She also relayed to Bush that the Saudi King's advisers had informed her that the funds for the no-confidence vote—which was defeated by twelve votes—had come from a Saudi businessman called bin Laden.

During Benazir's time as prime minister, Zardari and some associates were accused of benefiting from kickbacks, which earned him the nickname "Mr. Ten Percent." In a 2002 interview Bhutto admitted that her husband was "not an angel." He "associated with certain people, which gave him a bad name. I think my husband also had a different view about patronage than what is now acceptable," she declared; at the same time, she defended him, denying he had broken the law or stolen money.[15] Benazir was also accused of being a deficient manager and indecisive. Her disagreements with the president and the army over personnel matters led to the perception that she was not in charge.

Her government was dismissed in August 1990 by President Ishaq Khan under a controversial Eighth Amendment provision to the constitution, which dated from the Zia era, giving the president the power to dismiss the prime minister. Benazir was charged with corruption—for which, however, she was never tried—and for the inability to maintain law and order in the face of ethnic and sectarian violence. "The Military Intelligence was conspiring against my government from the first day,"[16] declared Benazir in a press conference the day after her demotion. This was becoming the norm of politics in Pakistan: presidents dismissing prime ministers on corruption charges and ousted leaders accusing intelligence agencies of interference in governmental affairs.

Nawaz Sharif came to power in the 1990 elections, backed by the Islamic Jamhoori Ittehad (IJI), an alliance of conservative and religious parties created and funded by the ISI. Benazir became leader of the opposition. Sharif's government was more pro-business than Benazir's, and he, as a Zia loyalist, continued giving significant political space to Islamic groups. He publicly declared that the army should have nothing to do with politics, but the prime minister sought to influence army matters surreptitiously. More importantly, Sharif attempted to reduce the president's powers, and in April 1993, President Khan dismissed him as prime minister, again under the Eighth Amendment provision, for the usual reasons: corruption and misadministration. Surprisingly, a month later, the Supreme Court overturned the president's decision and reinstalled Nawaz Sharif as prime minister. A couple of months later, the army forced both Sharif and President Khan to resign.

BENAZIR RETURNED TO power in the October 1993 elections, retaking her unfinished reform agenda as prime minister. Critics objected to Bhutto's designation of her husband, Asif Ali Zardari, to a cabinet post in the government.

An assassination attempt befell Benazir in the fall of 1993. Ramzi Yousef, a terrorist with ties to the ISI and nephew of Al-Qaida leader Khalid Sheikh Mohammed, placed a bomb in front of Benazir's house with the intention of activating it by remote control as she drove out of her garage. The attempt was frustrated as passing policemen drove Yousef away. Benazir recalled in her autobiography that a more elaborate plan involving Yousef, Al-Qaida, and the intelligence agencies—which failed for logistical reasons—"was based on assassinating me and making it look like my brother [Mir Murtaza] was responsible."[17]

The relationship between Benazir and her brother Mir Murtaza had been growing strained for years. Benazir considered her brother a political novice. While she was in jail, Benazir learned of her brother's role in the hijacking of a Pakistani passenger plane in which a passenger had been shot. The Al-Zulfikar group, an organization led by Mir Bhutto, claimed responsibility. Benazir criticized the incident. She felt it played into Zia's strategy of heightened confrontation to offset growing domestic dissatisfaction with the dictatorship.

Benazir and Mir Murtaza strongly disagreed on anti-Zia tactics. "Only violence can answer violence," Mir advocated, while Benazir favored peaceful struggle and mobilization to enable elections. In 1993, Mir rejected the conditions imposed by the military on the PPP government to stay out of defense sector decisions and not meddle with the ISI, while Benazir saw that there was no other choice and that realpolitik dictated the need to accept such limitations to her government's powers. Their differences were so marked that they had decided not to discuss politics during family gatherings.[18]

Mir Murtaza was still in exile, anxious to return to Pakistan. Benazir opposed the idea, however, because it would raise political problems for her, since her brother still faced judicial charges brought against him by the Zia regime. The prime minister told Mir that it was unknown how many cases were still open against him, as she had been informed that the ISI had "lost his file."[19]

Benazir saw her future aligned with the West, while domestically she would have to get along with the powers that be, including the ISI, the religious groups, and the entrepreneurial class—that is, the so-called establishment.

Bhutto became an active and founding member of the Council of Women World Leaders, a network of current and former prime ministers and presidents. Despite voicing concern for women's social and health issues, she failed to propose domestic legislation to empower women. Benazir's relations with the Supreme Court became strained when it reversed her appointment of twenty new judges to the Punjab High Court, some of whom were known as her party sympathizers. Benazir's political rival Nawaz Sharif hardened his opposition to the prime minister when her government jailed Sharif's aged father on charges of fraud.

By 1993, Mir Murtaza decided he had to return to Pakistan. Benazir had refused to give him and his group slots to run for congressional elections on the PPP ticket and had recommended that he "leave Syria, a rogue state in her estimation, and settle in London for a few years."[20] She had spoken to Margaret Thatcher about the possibility of him moving to London, and the British leader had agreed. But Mir had been reluctant to move. Instead, he had decided to run for office as an independent, and won. By then Mir had become an open critic of his sister's government and of the corruption associated with Benazir's husband, Asif Ali Zardari.

When Mir Murtaza landed in Karachi, after flying from Damascus via Dubai (as the government of Islamabad initially refused to allow the Syrian presidential plane carrying him to land), he was arrested and ended up spending eight months in jail. The charges included crimes related to the 1981 hijacking case of the Pakistan International Airlines plane that had left one passenger dead. He was now an opponent to the government led by his sister Benazir.[21]

Mir was eventually released, although cases against him remained active in court, which forced him to constantly appear at hearings. He toured Pakistan, speaking on his usual topics—namely, the corruption of the PPP. Benazir, in turn, saw her brother as an immature radical, even portraying him as a "terrorist," particularly when he spoke against the government repression on ethnic Muhajirs in Sindh—a population that speaks Urdu as opposed to Sindhi and is supported by the ultra-nationalist Muhajir Quami Movement—in the context of growing ethnic violence.

Benazir and Mir Murtaza did not see each other after his return to Pakistan until May 1996. In 1995, Mir set up his own party, which he named the PPP (Shaheed Bhutto). Benazir left her brother untouched by the state apparatus, but she had many of his followers thrown in jail. The ISI made it clear to Mir's supporters that if they changed sides, they would be freed.

Mir Murtaza blamed Benazir's husband for his persecution. According to Raja Anwar, a former student leader and guerrilla companion of Mir in exile, Mir was convinced that "Benazir's negative attitude towards him was the result of Asif's influence. Mir had nothing but contempt for his brother-in-law, whom he considered unworthy of his sister."[22]

One time, during an informal meeting with brother-in-law Zardari, Mir and his guards grabbed Benazir's husband and shaved off half of his iconic mustache, forcing Zardari to shave off the other half, to the delight of Mir's friends and the media.[23] Just before his death, Mir had happened to be with Zardari on the same flight from Islamabad to Karachi. After arriving at the airport, Mir's armed guards followed and harassed Asif, aiming their automatic weapons from their cars at the prime minister's husband. Zardari was terrified and, instead of going to his house, changed direction and went to his father's home. Once inside, Zardari phoned Abdullah Shah, chief minister of Sindh, and gave him hell for improper protection. He then learned that the police had been looking for one of Mir's top lieutenants.[24]

Mir Murtaza died in front of the Bhutto house at 70 Clifton in Karachi on the night of September 20, 1996, after being shot by policemen who had supposedly come to arrest him. The streetlights had been turned off. Gunfire broke out, with the police killing three of Mir's guards and wounding several others. Mir was shot several times. Two policemen were injured, though by their own actions, as forensic examinations later proved. The only spent ammunition came from police-issued weapons. Fatima Bhutto, Mir Murtaza's daughter, describes the last moments of her father's life in her moving memoir, *Songs of Blood and Sword*: "The last shot, Papa's autopsy showed, was fired into his jaw at point-blank range. . . . The street outside our house was hosed clean; all the blood and glass was [*sic*] washed away. By the time Mummy and I left the house at around 8.45, some fifteen minutes later, the police had removed all the evidence."[25]

The prime minister flew that same night from Islamabad to Karachi and went to the hospital where her brother had been taken for the autopsy, accompanied by a couple of police officers who had been at the scene of the shooting. She was weeping and barefoot, a sign of respect for her deceased brother. In her autobiography, Benazir claimed that she was particularly "distraught because [they had] just reconciled after some years of political estrangement."[26]

Considering the widespread rumors and accusations implicating Benazir and her husband in the gangland-style execution of Mir Murtaza,[27] the prime minister invited a team of former Scotland Yard detectives, led by Roy Herridge, to conduct their own independent investigation of the case. The interim report found evidence of a police conspiracy and of an unidentified gunman at the scene. The Herridge team was paid and invited to leave Pakistan by President Farooq Leghari after he had removed Benazir as prime minister. With Benazir out of office, the government no longer made deciphering Mir's assassination a priority.

In November 1996, several converging storms sank the Bhutto administration. First, corruption scandals involved Zardari, which eventually landed him in jail. Second, ethnic violence flared between native Sindhis and the Muhajir refugees from India and their descendants. Then, the hypothetical imposition of an agricultural tax, agreed by the Bhutto government and the International Monetary Fund, met with the strong opposition of the powerful landed elite. Mir Murtaza's scandalous murder was the last straw. President Farooq Leghari, a PPP member, invoked the Eighth Amendment to dismiss Benazir as prime minister, while rejecting her accusation—which she later denied—that both the army and the presidency were behind Mir's murder.

The Mir Murtaza case was never solved. One version of the events stated that his guards had fired first and killed Mir Murtaza accidentally in the alleged cross fire. Benazir's government opposed Mir's relatives' intention to file a criminal case against the police and, instead, set up a judicial inquiry into the case. The tribunal, although not empowered to pass sentences, established that there had been no shootout or cross fire and that the police had used excessive force and left the injured to die on the street.

Former interior minister general (ret.) Naseerullah Babar said that the ISI was involved in the murder of Mir Murtaza Bhutto. He affirmed that he had formed a commission to probe into the ISI role in the case but that pressure had mounted against the inquiry until it was dropped. Mir Murtaza's lawyers filed a criminal case in 1997 against Asif Ali Zardari, Abdullah Shah—the chief minister of Sindh Province—and two policemen for conspiracy to murder. Zardari was acquitted, and to this day, Mir Murtaza's death remains shrouded in mystery.

After Bhutto was deposed as prime minister, Nawaz Sharif returned to power following a decisive victory by his party in the February 1997 parliamentary elections. This time he moved quickly to curtail the powers of the presidency and the judiciary. The Parliament approved an amendment that removed the president's Eighth Amendment powers to dismiss the government.

Bhutto left Pakistan for Dubai in 1998 on a self-imposed exile. She kept her job as leader of the PPP during the following nine years. An important part of her activities during this long exile abroad was to fight the corruption charges leveled against her in Pakistan, as well as in Spain and Switzerland, and to secure the release from a Pakistani jail of her husband, who faced charges both for corruption and for his alleged involvement in the murder of Mir Murtaza Bhutto. Despite the documented accusations against Zardari—which were abundantly covered in numerous press reports, including a 1998 *New York Times* article entitled "House of Graft: Tracing the Bhutto Millions"[28]—she felt loyal to the father of her three children and her political partner. Some close advisers recommended abandoning him for the sake of her political career, but Benazir refused, standing by the man who had "presented her on their engagement with a ring engraved with the words: 'Until death do us part.'"[29] After all, some observers reflected, corruption was endemic in Pakistan, where government officials at the federal and local levels, generals, policemen, and business people all participated, to varying degrees, in corrupt practices.

In April 1999, a two-judge Ehtesab (accountability) Bench of the Lahore High Court convicted Benazir and her husband of corruption and sentenced them to five years in prison, fined them $8.6 million, and disqualified them from holding public office. The Ehtesab Bench had been set up by Nawaz Sharif—who made a businessman friend of his its president. Two years later, Pakistan's Supreme Court ruled that Benazir Bhutto's 1999 conviction had been biased and ordered a retrial.[30]

IN OCTOBER 1999, General Pervez Musharraf seized power from the democratically elected government of Prime Minister Nawaz Sharif in a dramatic coup d'état. Tension had been brewing between Sharif and the army ever since Musharraf had sent Pakistani mujahideen across the Line of Control in north Kashmir. The Kargil offensive, as it was known, provoked a forceful armed reaction from India, which threatened to escalate to full-out war. After the crisis subsided, the Sharif government announced Musharraf's dismissal, and on October 12, 1999, as the military chief flew back to Karachi from an official mission to Sri Lanka, they decided to keep him in exile by impeding his plane from landing at the Karachi airport.

At about 6:45 p.m., Pakistani International Airlines (PIA) flight 805 carrying Musharraf was informed that it would have to leave Pakistani airspace, even though it had only one hour and ten minutes of fuel remaining. Given the limited fuel, the plane had no option but to attempt to land in hostile India, and it was not at all clear that the plane would make it there safely. After several moments of extreme tension, Major General Malik Iftikhar Ali Khan, the commander of an army division in Karachi, rebelled and radioed the pilot, telling him that everything was all right and asking him to "tell the chief to come back and land in Karachi."[31] The army then arrested Sharif and several senior government officials, and the PIA flight finally landed in Karachi, with Musharraf as the new de facto leader of Pakistan.

Sharif, the deposed prime minister, was convicted in April 2000 on charges of hijacking an aircraft and treason and sentenced to life imprisonment. But after a year in jail, he was pardoned and sent off into exile to Saudi Arabia at the request of the Saudi royal family. Sharif was disqualified from public office for twenty-one years and was required to forfeit about $9 million in properties. The Musharraf regime also pursued renewed corruption investigations against Bhutto and Zardari.

Nawaz Sharif and Benazir Bhutto, now both in exile, formed an alliance of opposition parties, the Alliance for the Restoration of Democracy, which held protest rallies in Pakistan that were brutally repressed. Musharraf referred to Bhutto and Sharif as "useless politicians." Bhutto responded from London that the Pakistani army was "infected by extremists." By disqualifying the mainstream political leaders, she added, "the army plans a vacuum which can be filled by extremists linked to the Taliban."[32]

In June 2001, General Musharraf dismissed the president and assumed the presidential post himself while retaining the chief executive position and adding the new role of chief of army staff. He justified this dictatorial action as being "in the supreme national interest."[33]

In 2002, the general amended Pakistan's constitution to ban prime ministers from serving more than two terms, thus disqualifying both Bhutto and Sharif. With the opposition out of the way, Musharraf won the election of October 2002, legitimizing his rule. Beyond his electoral support, skewed though it may have been, General Musharraf had the backing of what is known in Pakistan as the Establishment—the de facto power structure whose permanent core is the military high command and intelligence agencies, in particular the powerful, military-run

ISI, as well as the MI and the Intelligence Bureau (IB). He had agreed with a coalition of Islamic parties to leave the army by December 31, 2004, and with such a promise, he mustered a two-thirds majority in Parliament to pass an amendment that retroactively legalized his 1999 coup and other decrees, although the general reneged on his word and kept his army post. The Parliament obliged by passing a bill enabling him to keep both offices.

By the time Musharraf took over, the post of prime minister had been suspended five times in Pakistan due to martial law or another form of military intervention, and no elected civilian prime minister had ever served a full five-year term. The military had been directly ruling the country for three of the six decades since independence.

The commissioners and staff of the UN Commission of Inquiry at the exact site at Liaquat Bagh, Rawalpindi, where Benazir Bhutto was killed, inspecting the area and interviewing senior policemen about the facts and circumstances of the assassination.

4

On the Road to Islamabad

"THE BHUTTO COMMISSION communications have been intercepted by an unknown party," Chief of Staff Mark Quarterman told me nervously a few hours before we were due to depart on our first visit to Pakistan. "A Pakistani government source has urgently contacted me to convey to you this information," Quarterman said. "Whoever intervened with our electronic mail knows about our agenda in Islamabad."

"We have to tell the UN Department of Safety and Security and seek their opinion," I replied.

When we contacted the department, known as the DSS, they asked us to consider suspending the trip. I felt this was overly cautious.

"Look, anyone could be interested in finding out about our communications—not just Pakistanis," I told our chief of staff. "I intend to go ahead."

It was July 14, 2009. Since we were scheduled to leave for Pakistan that day, we decided to revisit the issue with the DSS during our stopover in Dubai en route from New York to Islamabad.

At the Dubai airport, after our long and tiring trip, the DSS agreed that we should proceed to Pakistan but advised us not to leave the security perimeter in Islamabad known as the "red zone." Because any hotel or place of public access would represent a high security risk for the commissioners, we would be staying at the Sindh House, a residence for high officials from Sindh Province during their journeys to Islamabad. The Ministry of the Interior had been able to secure that venue for our commission during our visits. The Sindh House wasn't the ideal safe house available—the better-equipped one was the Punjab House—but Sindh offered the best security conditions according to an advance team that had evaluated the options. On every mission, newspapers in Pakistan reported that "strict security measures were in place at the Benazir Bhutto International Airport (in Islamabad) as the U.N. team arrived."[1]

The strong recommendation by the DSS not to leave the "red zone" of Islamabad was highly problematic. For reasons inherent to the nature of the inquiry, as well as for symbolic motives, we needed to visit the site of Benazir's assassination in Rawalpindi, a suburb of the Pakistani capital. I decided we had to go to Rawalpindi. Decoy plans—different times of departure for Rawalpindi, as well as different means of transportation—would be made to deceive anyone interested in harming us.

The mission we were embarking upon was particularly difficult because we didn't know what we were up against. Certainly, there were some political actors openly opposed to our investigation. We also anticipated possible resistance and obstruction within sectors close to the army and the ISI secret service.

An article in the *Guardian* summarized the challenge we were facing: "The three-man unit . . . will find themselves plunged into a murky work of conspiracy theories, power politics and conflicting agendas."[2] Indeed, Bhutto's assassination was steeped in controversy. But the *Guardian* did not go far enough. The commission soon encountered a country deeply skeptical of authority and the justice system because of widespread corruption, abundant behind-the-scenes political deal making, and the regular impunity that had met previous unsolved political assassinations.

UPON OUR ARRIVAL in Islamabad in the early hours of Thursday, July 16, the Pakistani government prepared a hospitable reception at our safe house and deployed for us a heavy antiterrorist security detail. Several UN policemen accompanied the commissioners for "close protection." During our first few hours in Islamabad, I was shocked to learn that our affable non-English-speaking cook at the Sindh House knew in detail our agenda in the Pakistani capital. I complained to our chief of staff and to an aide to the minister of the interior who acted as our contact person in the Pakistani government. No convincing explanation was ever given, except that the cook had to be aware about when we would be around to prepare the daily meals.

The work of our inquiry commission had begun in early July 2009, when the three commissioners and the full staff had gathered in New York for planning sessions and meetings with high UN officials and with the ambassador of Pakistan to the United Nations, Abdullah Haroon, and his aides. Our priority had been to firm up our program for the first visit to Pakistan from July 15 to 18, 2009. We had entrusted administrative and logistic details to our able staff.

The first visit to Islamabad began with a meeting with our chief contact in the Pakistani government and one of the principal advocates of the investigation, Interior Minister Rehman Malik. He was the key interlocutor in our investigation not only as the official point of contact in the government but also as the ex–security adviser of Benazir Bhutto and one of the close aides who had accompanied her on the day of the murder.

Malik was born in 1951 in a town north of Lahore, had earned a doctorate in criminology, and had spent nearly three decades in the Federal Investigation Agency, rising to the top during Bhutto's second term as prime minister. Sacked and jailed by the Nawaz Sharif government in 1998, he had emerged as Benazir's principal security adviser while both were in exile in London. According to one source, Malik became a business partner of Benazir, and both were investigated by a Spanish court, which was looking into a company they were associated with called Petroline FZC, "which had made questionable payments to Iraq under Saddam Hussein."[3]

Rehman Malik resembled an Italian actor from a B movie. Graced with jet-black curly hair and sporting a mustache, he dressed sharply in impeccable suits—colorful ties, silk handkerchiefs regularly adorning the front jacket pocket—and pointed leather shoes. His capacity for hard work impressed us. On several occasions, we met with him at midnight, conversed until two or three in the morning, and saw him again at breakfast by eight, where he appeared fresh and ready while we struggled with jet lag and exhaustion due to lack of sleep.

We met Minister Malik at his office in a compound of government buildings. Instead of a working meeting across a table, Minister Malik received us in a formal setting of two rows of chairs—us on one side, his advisers on the other—with the minister in the middle.

On this first meeting at the Ministry of the Interior, Malik expressed his satisfaction with the United Nations having agreed to conduct this investigation and with our personal commitment to carry out this challenging duty on behalf of Secretary-General Ban Ki-moon. Much to our astonishment, Minister

Malik informed us that their own internal investigation had made great strides, that the police had confessions from four individuals accused of Benazir's murder, and that they were in custody.

"I think your work will be made easy when you read this document," Minister Malik said as he handed me a bound report entitled *Summary of Investigation and Trial Conducted So Far for UN Fact-Finding Commission.* The seventy-page report was dated June 20, 2009, signed by the Ministry of the Interior, and labeled "Restricted."

"Thanks; I'm sure this will be very useful," I responded while I quickly leafed through a few pages and saw that the index included annexes such as witness statements, a summary of the Scotland Yard report, a list of seized articles at the crime scene, names of court judges, special prosecutors, defense lawyers, and so forth.

"This is very complete," Malik added. "This is your own report ready to be issued, of course, with the changes and additions that you may see fit."

I looked at my fellow commissioners in puzzlement. The interior minister was handing us what he expected would be the draft final report of the Commission of Inquiry. In short, his message was that our investigation could very well conclude there and then; we did not have to bother with any detailed inquiry. It was a sign of things to come.

Our relationship with Minister Malik was rocky. He never satisfactorily answered our questions about his role and actions during the moments surrounding Bhutto's assassination. Our insistence on checking details—for example, the distance between his vehicle and the scene of the crime at the moment of the attack—clearly made him uncomfortable. Malik informed us that he had received important information from a "brotherly country" about serious threats to Benazir Bhutto and himself; but despite our requests, he never furnished the details of those threats. On other occasions, he would provide us with incomplete information to be developed at a next conversation.

The minister was always cordial and courteous, dispensing gifts after every visit, which, as we told him, we could not accept due to United Nations ethics rules. He insisted, and those fine gifts ended up in the care of the UN Ethics Office in New York City.

We had a disagreement with the Ministry of the Interior about the quality of our protection during our second visit when the antiterrorist police contingent was replaced by nonspecialized security troops who would point their automatic rifles at our vehicles, instead of upwards or at the floor, when riding in the protection trucks in front of us. Our complaints were generally accommodated; but a few months after the start of our work, we did not feel as warmly welcomed as we did at the outset.

On our first day of work, we paid a visit to Benazir Bhutto's widower and president of Pakistan, Asif Ali Zardari. He had been named cochairman of the PPP after Benazir's murder and had immediately demanded a UN probe into the crime.

After the PPP leader's assassination, the parliamentary elections scheduled for January 8, 2008, for which she was campaigning, were postponed to February 2008. The PPP allied with the Pakistan Muslim League-Nawaz (PML-N), led by Nawaz Sharif, and emerged victorious. The new coalition put forth Yousuf Raza Gilani as prime minister. Musharraf's position became increasingly untenable, and he resigned the presidency in August to avoid impeachment procedures in Parliament. Zardari was then thrust from being an operator behind the scenes, and a political partner of his wife, to president of Pakistan after winning the electoral college contest in September 2008. In the meantime, the Pakistani government had officially contacted the UN secretary-general to request the establishment of a commission to probe Bhutto's assassination.

During that July 2009 visit to Zardari, heavy security slowed our access to the presidential palace. Despite a courteous treatment by presidential staff, we had to leave our cell phones at a guard station for security reasons. Later, a high official apologized, explaining that in our case such overzealousness had been unwarranted.

The commissioners and our chief of staff sat in a row of chairs across from a row with several key ministers and Bhutto and President Zardari's children. In the middle was the presidential chair. Zardari was cordial and appreciative about the establishment of the commission and our personal involvement. He explained the importance of our investigative work for his family and for Pakistan. The president reminded us that from the very beginning, immediately after the assassination of his wife, he had requested an impartial investigation conducted by the United Nations.

Much of the conversation was general, as the formal context did not allow for any in-depth queries about the facts we were interested in. I outlined our program of interviews, which included policemen, witnesses, authorities, and representatives of civil society. I told the president that we intended to visit the scene of the crime in Rawalpindi. The children, including PPP chairman Bilawal, followed the dialogue attentively but did not intervene.

We requested a private conversation with President Zardari to inquire about key facts relevant to our work. He accommodated us on at least two further occasions; our interviews included a lengthy and emotionally charged question-and-answer session at his suite at the InterContinental Hotel in Manhattan during his attendance at the September 2009 General Debate of the UN General Assembly in New York.

VISITING THE SCENE of the crime was complicated. As it involved leaving the "red zone," we made fake arrangements to go by helicopter the following day—Friday, July 17—in the afternoon. We even put the details in our updated agenda. Instead, we left at 5:00 a.m. in a caravan of vehicles to avoid detection by anyone interested in blocking our work or harming us and to avoid the press that followed us everywhere.

The roads to Rawalpindi had little traffic, and they actually looked deserted, as the police blocked cross streets along our route for us. At Liaquat Bagh, the park where Benazir was assassinated, we expected to meet senior Rawalpindi police officers who had firsthand information about the events of December 27, 2007.

When we arrived at Liaquat Bagh, we found that the police had cordoned off a two-block perimeter. As we got out of our vehicles, I noticed a small crowd about two blocks away, behind police barriers. Peter Fitzgerald, the Irish commissioner, pointed out what was going on: "It's the press, Heraldo. There are bunches of them." In fact, we could see the cameras and telephoto lenses pointed toward us. Someone had tipped off the press about the exact time we would be at Liaquat Bagh.

The senior police officers guided us along the course that Benazir had taken to enter the parking lot and the back of the platform from where she had addressed the crowd. We went up the wooden steps, and I walked around where the dais would have been located that day. From there I commanded a good view of the entire park and the adjacent buildings. I saw sharpshooters on nearby rooftops who had been posted for our security. A Thai UN policeman in charge of my close protection promptly asked me to leave the platform. "This is not safe. You are too exposed," he said.

We descended into the parking lot and walked the path Bhutto had followed out of Liaquat Bagh and stopped at the exact spot of her assassination. We asked many questions: Why had she turned right instead of left as originally planned? Why was the access to the left blocked? What preventive work had been done before her arrival? How many policemen and police vehicles were escorting her? Why were there so many people around her vehicle? Our staff took abundant notes. The policemen gave ample explanations that attempted to show they had done their job. Our retired Irish deputy police chief, Peter Fitzgerald, was skeptical. If everything had been so perfect, why then had the prime minister been assassinated? he asked me. We announced to the Pakistani officials that we needed to interrogate the Rawalpindi police officers separately during our visit.

Local media provided abundant coverage of our visit to Rawalpindi. The newspaper *The Nation* wrote that "amid tight security," the UN commission team "parked a vehicle as was used by Benazir Bhutto at the time of assassination and examined the killing scene." Then, the news story continued, "the team also examined the nearby buildings and trees at Liaquat Bagh. The U.N. officials took snaps of the site and made sketches, and also examined the stage where Benazir Bhutto had delivered her last address."[4]

We found many witnesses of the crime—politicians, diplomats, friends of Benazir Bhutto, and members of civil society—more than willing to cooperate, providing us with their testimony, opinions, and hypotheses about the murder. Military officials and policemen tended to be cautious and, in some cases, were visibly edgy about speaking to the commission. But some active and retired intelligence officials were much more forthcoming. At the Sindh House, where we conducted the more sensitive interviews, we saw high uniformed officials become agitated and perspire profusely as they attempted to answer our queries. One fellow commissioner, former Indonesian attorney general Marzuki Darusman, was particularly calm about asking incisive questions and pointing out contradictions. The Rawalpindi policemen's behavior shifted from initial arrogance and self-assuredness to defensive nervousness as we pressed them with detailed questions. "This guy is lying," our former Irish cop announced at one point when Police Chief Saud Aziz repeatedly changed parts of his testimony or suddenly recalled facts he had claimed to have forgotten only after we presented him with evidence we already possessed.

Toward the end of the first visit, the commission's media adviser, Ben Malor, counseled us to give a press conference to satisfy media curiosity and avoid speculation. The press conference, held at the Serena Hotel, attracted about six dozen journalists from media outlets around the world. As chairman of the commission, I gave a brief statement explaining the nature of our mandate. I hoped to lower expectations somewhat. The odds were against us that we would be able to identify culprits. As I told the journalists, our plan was to conduct interviews on a voluntary basis in Pakistan and abroad as needed. Then I described our agenda of official meetings during that first visit, thanked the government for providing us with detailed materials, and emphasized that since ours was not a criminal investigation, it was up to the competent Pakistani institutions to establish responsibilities in the crime. I also stressed that our work would be guided by objectivity, independence, and professionalism. Many questions were posed, some that revealed skepticism about the eventual outcome of the commission's inquiry. Only one or two questions suggested a veiled hostility, including one about whether we would interview fugitive Taliban leader Baitullah Mehsud.

SECURITY ISSUES SURROUNDED our visits to Pakistan. After the July visit, I had a conversation, accompanied by our commission's chief of staff, with UN under-secretary-general for security and safety Gregory Starr, who analyzed our task with cold-blooded realism: "You have the best possible security, but nothing is fail-safe," he said. "The bulletproof car that is being provided for you in Pakistan is an armored B6 level vehicle, which will resist high-powered rifle fire. But, of course, if a suicide bomber with an explosives jacket wraps himself around your car, there is no protection that will keep you safe."

Between our second and third visit to Pakistan, on October 5, 2009, a suicide bomber wearing an improvised explosive device and dressed in a uniform of the Frontier Constabulary, a Pakistani paramilitary force, made his way past the security perimeter and into the offices of the UN World Food Program (UNWFP), where he detonated his device. Five UNWFP employees were killed and six others were injured. The Tehrik-i-Taliban Pakistan (TTP), the same group that had successfully attacked the Pearl Continental Hotel in Peshawar in June using a vehicle-borne improvised explosive device, later claimed responsibility for the attack.

Not only was our mission controversial and dangerous in the eyes of some Pakistani sectors, but jihadist leaders had been targeting the United Nations as an infidel organization. In an April 2008 speech, Al-Qaida's second-in-command, Ayman al-Zawahiri, had declared, "The United Nations is an enemy of Islam and Muslims. It is the one which codified and legitimized the establishment of the state of Israel and its taking over of the Muslims' lands."[5]

As the work of the commission progressed, some interests in Pakistan apparently came to view it as menacing. Prior to our third visit in February 2010, our invitation to use the Sindh House was withdrawn, supposedly due to a request by the governor of Sindh. After we protested to Minister Malik, the house was again placed at our disposal. Commissioner Marzuki Darusman's flight via state-owned Pakistan International Airlines from Jakarta to Islamabad was canceled, causing him to miss that third visit; some Pakistanis interpreted the cancellation as having been intentional.

In early February 2010, as we prepared to wind down our investigative work, we received a disquieting message from a credible friendly source in Pakistan: "The commissioners' security may be in danger. These people are thugs and they are capable of anything if it fits their interests. Besides, they are parochial and don't know how the world operates." We never learned who "these people" referred to, but we had an idea and took due note of the warning.

Information leaks plagued our work. After the October 2009 suicide attack on the UNWFP offices, the UN Department of Safety and Security strongly advised that we postpone our third visit scheduled for November. We decided to follow the department's advice and, to our surprise, a detailed article about the suspension of our visit appeared in the Pakistani media. The article included quotes from a confidential note we had sent to the Islamabad government requesting that arrangements be made for us to interview General Pervez Musharraf.[6]

Assuming that the Sindh House would have hidden listening devices, our commission team often walked around the gardens of the premises, sometimes in the scorching sun, to discuss some of the more delicate issues we encountered in our inquiry or to adopt decisions that needed to remain secret.

On the Road to Islamabad

As we departed after our initial visit, protocol officials accompanied us to the airport VIP lounge. One individual, whom I remembered seeing during our arrival and who identified himself as a "diplomatic liaison," approached me when I was seated looking over papers and, after expressing that he hoped we had had a good visit, asked me who I thought had committed Benazir Bhutto's assassination.

"Look, we just began our inquiry," I said, trying to be courteous, "and as you know, it's not up to us to identify culprits."

"Yes, I understand. But do you at least have any sense about who might have done it?" he insisted.

"As I said, this is not part of our work," I replied, a bit annoyed.

"But just think of it as a hypothesis: What's your best hunch about who might have perpetrated the murder?"

It was such an obvious ploy to gather intelligence that I simply stood up and walked away to join the rest of the team members on the other end of the room.

When, aboard the plane, I told my colleagues about the disagreeable dialogue I had just had with the "diplomatic liaison" in the VIP room, one of them told me he had experienced exactly the same interrogation from the same individual. We never saw the "diplomatic liaison" again on any of our subsequent visits.

President George W. Bush and Pakistani president Pervez Musharraf shake hands after concluding a joint press conference in Islamabad, during a visit of the US president to Pakistan on March 4, 2006.

5

The US Gravitas in Pakistani Affairs

As the irony of history would have it, on the morning of September 11, 2001, General Mahmood Ahmed, the director general of Pakistan's secret intelligence service, the ISI, was on Capitol Hill meeting with Porter Goss, chairman of the Senate Intelligence Committee. General Ahmad was there explaining that Pakistan was doing its best to convince the Taliban to hand over Osama bin Laden to US authorities.

The ISI had cultivated deep ties with the Taliban as a way of countering the growing influence of India and Russia in Afghanistan. It was Pakistan, through its military, that had provided the Taliban fighters with the support and assistance that had allowed them to seize power in the mid-1990s, dislodging the Northern Alliance–dominated Afghan government. Now, the 9/11 attacks and the subsequent US reaction obliged Pakistan to make a choice: either sever ties with the Taliban and support the US efforts in Afghanistan or face American wrath.

Secretary of State Colin Powell phoned Musharraf the day

after 9/11, around 1:30 p.m., with a straightforward message: "You are either with us or against us." Deputy Secretary of State Richard Armitage received ISI director Ahmed that same day at 10 a.m. at the State Department and he was even more blatant with the visiting Pakistani spymaster: Pakistani authorities had to choose between the United States and the terrorists, and if they chose the latter, they had to be prepared to be "bombed back to the Stone Age."[1] When General Ahmed returned the next day to the State Department for a second meeting with the deputy secretary of state, he was handed a list of seven specific demands of cooperation. "This is not negotiable," Armitage warned. The general, known to be sympathetic to the Taliban, quickly read the sheet of paper and replied that all the demands were acceptable. "Don't you want to discuss it with your president?" Armitage asked. "I know the president's mind," responded the ISI chief, who had phoned Musharraf the night before to convey Washington's mood.[2] Indeed, General Musharraf chose cooperation. Anything else would have almost certainly meant military action by the United States and a deepening US-India alliance in the region.

On September 13, the American ambassador in Islamabad, Wendy Chamberlin, personally delivered to Musharraf the same list of seven demands from Washington regarding Al-Qaida, the Taliban, and "domestic expressions of support for terrorism against the United States."[3] As General Ahmed had anticipated, Musharraf accepted them.

This was by no means the first time the United States tried to shape Pakistan's political life. In fact, America has been a fundamental factor in Pakistan's foreign and domestic affairs from the very founding of the country. When, in 2007, Washington put pressure on Musharraf and Benazir Bhutto to induce a power-sharing arrangement, it was only one of the latest expressions of the United States' ubiquity in Pakistan's political landscape.

PAKISTAN'S ATTITUDE TOWARD the United States was shaped soon after independence. Although Washington had favored a united India and was unenthusiastic about the idea of Pakistan, Muhammad Ali Jinnah, Pakistan's founder and first governor-general, felt very close to the United States. As early as September 1947, Jinnah had told his cabinet that Pakistan as a democracy had to align "with the UK and the USA rather than with Russia" and that, furthermore, "communism [did] not flourish in the soil of Islam."[4]

After Jinnah's untimely death on September 11, 1948, his successor Liaquat Ali Khan followed the same foreign policy line of alignment with Washington. In a meeting with US secretary of state George Marshall in October 1948, during the United Nations General Assembly, Liaquat assured his interlocutor that "communism [was] against Islam"[5] and urged Washington to deliver economic aid to the new nation as it was doing across Europe after World War II.

In 1950, Prime Minister Liaquat backed the American decision to invoke UN collective security action against the North Korean invasion. Pakistan lobbied the US position with Middle Eastern and South Asian countries, but it stopped short of sending troops to Korea, as Liaquat felt his country needed a security guarantee against India. Washington viewed South Asia as a region marginal to the intensifying Cold War, except for specific areas of conflict such as Afghanistan and Kashmir. In contrast, from the Pakistani side, the top priority was not the Cold War or communism but the dispute with India in general and specifically over Kashmir.

Following the murder of Liaquat, the succeeding leaders continued to voice Pakistan's endorsement of the anticommunist cause and willingness to join the so-called free world's security system. "Our army can be your army if you want us,"[6] said General Ayub Khan to a high State Department official during a visit to Washington DC in September 1953.

President Dwight Eisenhower and his secretary of state, John Foster Dulles, were understandably sympathetic to Karachi's foreign policy postures. Dulles disliked India's nonalignment and viewed a well-armed Pakistani army as a stronghold against the Soviet threat. Vice President Richard Nixon enthusiastically supported the idea of helping Pakistan as, from his visits to New Delhi and Karachi, he had emerged with negative perceptions of India and positive ones of Pakistan. In a briefing to the National Security Council after a trip to Asia in 1953, Nixon declared that Pakistan was "a country I would like to do everything for."[7]

Not surprisingly, the United States under Eisenhower decided to arm Pakistan as part of a scheme to defend the Middle East and South Asia against the Soviets. On May 19, 1954, Pakistan and the United States signed a Mutual Defense Assistance Agreement that provided the foundation for the provision of military aid. Pakistan's alignment with the West was sharply criticized by Third World nonaligned countries, but Karachi felt it had struck a good deal with Washington. In 1955 Pakistan joined the seven-country Southeast Asia Treaty Organization (SEATO), a largely political organization modeled after NATO but lacking its automatic military mechanism against aggression. Later, Pakistan joined the Baghdad Pact and its successor CENTO (the Central Treaty Organization). The main security reason Pakistan joined these pacts was to strengthen its hand in requesting US military assistance and to claim, as General Ayub

Khan did, that Pakistan had become Washington's "most allied ally in Asia."[8]

The Soviet endorsement of New Delhi's posture on Kashmir, accompanied by a sizable package of economic and military aid to Afghanistan in late 1955, further convinced Pakistanis that alignment with the United States was vital. Pakistan felt confident of Washington's friendship as it leaned toward free enterprise policies, while India opted for a state-oriented approach to economic development.

Pakistan's internal instability led Washington to occasionally warn the country's leaders about the need to stick to the democratic political processes. But in a Cold War context, the United States valued disciplined and efficient leadership such as that provided by General Ayub Khan, who took over in a bloodless coup in late 1958. A US-Pakistan bilateral security agreement was signed in 1959 as further proof of the ongoing cooperation between the two countries. During his second term, in December 1959, Eisenhower became the first American president to visit Pakistan.

In 1959 Pakistan agreed to grant the US Air Force a ten-year lease to establish a communications facility at Badaber, near Peshawar, the capital of the North-West Frontier Province, as a cover for a major intercept operation run by the National Security Agency. At the same time, the CIA was granted permission to fly U-2 spy planes from Peshawar over the Soviet Union.

The downing of a US spy plane over Russia in 1960 and the capture of its pilot, Gary Powers, demonstrated to the Pakistanis the costs of aligning with Washington, as the country became openly entangled in the East-West conflict. Within Ayub's cabinet, a young minister from Sindh Province by the name of Zulfikar Ali Bhutto strongly advocated for a more independent relationship with the United States and for improved ties with the Soviet Union and China.

Ayub was a pragmatist who sided with Washington so long as the American administration, then presided over by John Kennedy, would not align with India's positions or provide it with military assistance. When Bhutto became foreign minister, the US government considered him to be pro-Chinese and anti-American.

When Bhutto attended the Kennedy funeral in Washington on November 25, 1963, he had a brief encounter with President Lyndon Johnson in which the foreign minister announced that he had an important personal message from Ayub. Johnson inquired what the message was, but Bhutto responded he didn't have it with him and would need an additional meeting to deliver it. Tied up with interviews with more than a hundred heads of state or high officials who had attended the funeral, the president was irritated by the request but made time for a meeting at the Oval Office. Bhutto then delivered a message from Ayub containing nothing of such substance as to justify a special interview. After a few pleasantries, Bhutto assumed it was time to leave and got up. An angry Johnson instructed Bhutto to sit down and lectured him on the growing bilateral tensions. Bhutto attempted to explain Pakistan's intense feelings regarding India, but Johnson cut him off and warned that problems would arise if Pakistan deepened its links with China. Johnson added that the United States was "indeed a friend of Pakistan and would continue to be one if Pakistan would let [it]."[9] Bhutto left the White House visibly shaken and upset. From there on, US-Pakistani relations soured further as Pakistan protested a US arms deal with India and refused to accommodate American requests for assistance in the Vietnam War effort, which, in the eyes of President Johnson, was equivalent to Pakistan ignoring its alliance obligations with Washington. The Pakistan-US alliance had become, in Dennis Kux's words, a "national affair."[10]

THE POSITIVE RELATIONSHIP between Pakistan and the United States was renewed with Richard Nixon in the White House and Yahya Khan, who had fought in World War II, as the ruler of Islamabad. In the summer of 1969, President Nixon became the second American president to visit Pakistan. Nixon expressed his intention to restore a relationship of friendship with Pakistan, based on mutual interests. More importantly, Nixon trusted Yahya in facilitating a secret dialogue process with China that would evolve into the historic opening of relations between the United States and China, inaugurated by Nixon's visit to Beijing in February 1972.

Nixon and Kissinger felt a debt of gratitude toward Pakistan. Both leaders also preferred Pakistan to India. "The Indians are no goddamn good," said Nixon to Kissinger as they discussed the 1971 Pakistan-India war over East Pakistan's secession. Kissinger agreed: "Those sons-of-bitches have never lifted a finger for us."[11] Unlike Indira Gandhi—whom Nixon personally disliked—they believed Yahya Khan to be a trustworthy soldier.

Declassified documents from the US National Archives and the Presidential Library system show that the White House had ordered a "tilt towards Pakistan," although Nixon had told congressional leaders that the United States was neutral in the conflict. Beyond Nixon's instruction to rule out putting public pressure on Pakistan, the tilt included secretly providing fighter planes to Pakistan through third parties, including F-5 fighter aircraft, which were originally slated for Libya but flown to Pakistan via Iran. It also involved the transfer of F-104s through Jordan and sending the nuclear-powered USS *Enterprise* to the Bay of Bengal as a warning to India.

After the East Pakistan conflict was over, Bhutto met with President Nixon at the White House. Bhutto told Nixon that Pakistan was "completely in the debt of the United States" and expressed that his days of anti-Americanism were over. Nixon promised to do everything possible to help Pakistan.[12]

On December 20, 1971, General Yahya Khan, having been militarily humiliated by India and having lost East Pakistan to independence, resigned and designated Bhutto as Pakistan's new president and chief martial law administrator. Bhutto had won the 1970 elections in West Pakistan, and now he had won the country. The victor took charge of a shaken and diminished nation.

President Gerald Ford, who succeeded Nixon after his resignation, singled out the nuclear issue as the key bilateral difference. Bhutto decided that Pakistan had to press ahead with its own nuclear program after India shook the world on May 8, 1974, by detonating an underground nuclear bomb. Kissinger, who stayed on as secretary of state, attempted to convince Bhutto to accept a muscular conventional arms package, including A-7 attack bombers, in exchange for giving up the nuclear road. But Bhutto refused to either cancel or postpone the nuclear project, which he put in the hands of A. Q. Khan[13] in late 1975.

The election of Jimmy Carter in 1976 changed the entire tone of the bilateral relationship. Abruptly, the cooperative, generally supportive, businesslike relationship was over. Kissinger, with whom Bhutto had forged personal ties, was now out of the picture. And Bhutto's growing domestic problems had an impact on the new administration in Washington.

The first signal of Washington's new attitude came in April 1977, when the State Department announced that it was blocking the export of tear gas to Pakistan on the grounds that such a sale would indicate US support for a "repressive regime." Intercepted telephone conversations between American diplomats in which coded reference was made to a source saying that "the party is over"[14] led Bhutto to accuse the United States of plotting to oust him from power. Bhutto launched an official protest, which resulted in a denial of the charges by Washington.

On July 5, 1977, when General Zia ul-Haq removed Bhutto and imposed martial law, US relations with Pakistan only worsened. Zulfikar Ali Bhutto was hanged on the morning of April 4, 1979, in Rawalpindi. Soon thereafter, the United States suspended aid to Pakistan. In 1977 the United States adopted the Glenn Amendment to the Foreign Assistance Act, which barred US aid to countries that had not signed the Nuclear Nonproliferation Treaty (NPT) and that imported nuclear fuel–reprocessing technology. Technically the suspension of aid came from Glenn Amendment violations, but many believed that the timing of the sanctions had to do with Zia's indifference to President Carter's and other world leaders' repeated clemency appeals for Bhutto's life.

Bilateral ties reached a new low with the November 1979 burning of the US embassy in Islamabad after rumors that the United States had been involved in the seizure of the Grand Mosque in Mecca. But things changed on Christmas Eve 1979, when the Soviet Union invaded Afghanistan to install an unconditional communist regime in Kabul.

AFTER THE SOVIET army invasion of Afghanistan, Carter called General Zia, reaffirmed the 1959 bilateral security agreement against communist aggression and offered further security assistance. The specifics of the assistance package to Pakistan added up to only $400 million, a figure dismissed by Zia as "peanuts," an apparent reference to Carter's previous occupation as a peanut farmer that irritated the American president.

At a less visible level, cooperation began to move much more swiftly. Four days after the Soviet invasion, President Carter approved a broad covert action program managed by the CIA to support Afghan resistance fighters. Zbigniew Brzezinski, the US national security adviser, became the key player behind the effort. The United States put its détente with the Soviet Union on hold and began to support Pakistan as a frontline state, despite being a dictatorial regime.

President Carter invited General Zia to the White House in October 1980, demonstrating that Pakistan, thanks to the Soviet intervention in Afghanistan, had shifted from international pariah to key Western ally.

Zia ul-Haq placed the ISI under the leadership of Lieutenant General Akhtar Abdur Rahman on center stage in the entire Afghanistan operation. Zia also phoned the Saudi Arabian king to set up a direct link between the ISI's General Akhtar and Prince Turki bin Faisal, the head of Saudi intelligence.[15] In addition, Saudi Arabia matched the funds provided by the CIA to the mujahideen through Pakistan. Strictly speaking, Pakistan was working with Afghan Islamists in covert operations inside Afghanistan well before the agreement with Washington. In fact, it was Zulfikar Ali Bhutto who charged the head of Pakistan's paramilitary Frontier Corps, Major General Naseerullah Babar, with the duty of training conservative Islamists to hit hard-line leftist nationalists. The Islamists activated by Bhutto and General Babar included Gulbuddin Hekmatyar, Burhanuddin Rabbani, and Ahmad Shah Massoud, who later became prominent commanders in the resistance against the Soviets.

General Babar would become, in 1994, interior minister in the government of Benazir Bhutto.

With the ascendancy of Ronald Reagan to the presidency, the American-Pakistani covert operation in Afghanistan grew considerably. A direct link was established between General Akhtar of the ISI and CIA director William Casey. An agreement was reached for a package of arms and supplies worth $3.2 billion over five years, to be handled and distributed exclusively by the ISI. Pakistan's intelligence would discipline, train, and coordinate the disparate mujahideen groups. In his characteristic fashion, "Zia maintained the façade of negotiations with the Soviets for a peaceful settlement"[16] and went through the motions of UN talks in Geneva.

Washington and Islamabad agreed that only the ISI would deal directly with the Afghan rebels. The CIA would train Pakistanis in the use of new military hardware, and the ISI, in turn, would instruct the Afghans. Taliban ambassador to Pakistan Abdul Salam Zaeef narrated in his memoir, *My Life with the Taliban*, that the ISI began to run a special weapons training program in the early 1980s for the mujahideen, in which he took part.[17] A pro-Taliban lobby was set up in Pakistan run by ISI retired officers and by active members of the army. The mujahideen established offices in Pakistan under the supervision of the ISI.

General Zia allowed only seven Afghan exiled political parties to operate from Pakistani territory, in Peshawar, and to receive CIA aid. According to Ahmed Rashid, "All seven were religion-based, as Zia forbade Afghan nationalist, democratic, or secular left-wing parties to operate from Pakistan. He insisted that the parties speak of the war as a jihad and not as a nationalist liberation movement."[18] The ISI favored one of the most extreme groups, led by Hekmatyar, a vehemently anti-American Islamist.

The Reagan-Zia partnership downplayed controversial issues in the bilateral relationship. The nuclear controversy would not become the central focus of US-Pakistani ties so long as Islamabad did not detonate a bomb. Moreover, as assured by Secretary of State Alexander Haig, human rights and democracy—unlike during the Carter administration—would now be viewed as an "internal problem" of the Pakistanis.

In December 1982, General Zia traveled to the United States on a state visit that reflected the renewed friendship between the two countries. Pakistan was receiving $600 million annually in military and economic aid, and Saudi Arabia was contributing matching amounts to the Afghan resistance. In the following years, high US officials routinely visited Islamabad and made side trips to Peshawar to publicly meet with Afghan refugees and tribal leaders.

In October 1986, President Reagan certified for the first time, under the so-called Pressler Amendment, that Pakistan did not possess a nuclear device. But nuclear program chief A. Q. Khan asserted the opposite in an interview, causing alarm in Washington. Khan said the country had achieved nuclear capability despite official Pakistani denials. Things were not made any easier for Islamabad when, in July 1987, a Canadian citizen of Pakistani origin was arrested in Philadelphia for illegally attempting to export maraging steel used to make atomic bomb casings. The *New York Times* published an editorial entitled "Punish Pakistan's Perfidy on the Bomb."[19] Despite the uproar over the nuclear issue, President Reagan used his waiver authority, citing national interest for not imposing sanctions against Pakistan.

In Afghanistan, the Soviets were making plans to leave the country. The mujahideen had made significant progress in their fighting after they had obtained US-made Stinger missiles, thanks largely to the lobbying of Congressman Charlie Wilson and a group of Pakistani and Afghan resistance supporters, who had convinced Reagan to provide them, despite the objections of the Pentagon, which feared the Stingers could fall into the hands of terrorists. The Stingers brought down the until-then almost invincible Soviet helicopters and changed the course of the war. On April 14, 1988, the Geneva Accords for the withdrawal of Soviet troops were signed by high officials of the United States, the Soviet Union, Pakistan, and Afghanistan.

The United States had secured its main objective of getting the Soviets out of Afghanistan. But General Zia held higher aspirations: he wanted to shape and control the nature of the government in Kabul. In fact, Zia had delayed the signing of the Geneva Accords so that he could maximize the flow of military hardware to the mujahideen, given that after the signing, neither Pakistan nor the Soviet Union could send more arms to Afghanistan. Zia's death unsettled this objective of gaining "strategic depth" in Afghanistan to counter India and to ensure a fundamentalist Islamic regime in Kabul.

BENAZIR BHUTTO RETURNED to Pakistan in 1986 to fight for democracy. To give a civilian varnish to his dictatorship, Zia named Muhammad Khan Junejo as prime minister. When Prime Minister Junejo began to assert himself in his post, however, even inviting Benazir Bhutto to a meeting to discuss the Geneva Accords, General Zia sacked him.

After Zia's death in an August 1988 plane crash, elections were held in November. Benazir beat Zia loyalist and businessman Nawaz Sharif despite the ISI's active support. The American government had advocated for fair elections, and after Benazir's win, Washington pressured the military into letting her assume office as prime minister.

Although Benazir's election as prime minister had a hugely positive political impact among both Republicans and Democrats in the US Congress, she had to respond to serious questions about her country's nuclear activity when she visited Washington to meet with President George H. W. Bush. In an address to a joint session of Congress, she declared, "We do not possess, nor do we intend to make, a nuclear device. This is our policy."[20] US officials doubted that she was part of the nuclear decision-making process, but she claimed she had forced her way into the loop, creating a triumvirate along with the other two key members of the government, President Ghulam Ishaq Khan and General Beg. In fact, it was thanks to a CIA briefing that Benazir had acquired enough information on the nuclear program in her country to assert herself as a relevant player in the governing troika.[21]

Benazir surrounded herself with American advisers, such as Peter Galbraith, her college friend, former staffer for Senator Claiborne Pell, and later ambassador to Croatia; Mark Siegel, Washington lobbyist; and Senator Daniel Patrick Moynihan. Their access to the prime minister was fluid—or excessive, according to the Pakistani ambassador to the United States, who wrote, "I was astounded to note the accessibility accorded to the Americans as they attended meetings in the prime minister's office and participated in the preparation of briefs. . . . Even matters as sensitive as the nuclear issue were raised in the discussions."[22]

On November 18, 1988, before leaving the White House, President Reagan had signed the latest certification under the Pressler Amendment that Pakistan did not possess a nuclear weapon. He had done so after intense debate among the various branches of government.[23] Benazir Bhutto began hearing heightened worries about Pakistan's nuclear program from her American interlocutors.

After the Soviet withdrawal from Afghanistan in 1989, the Mohammad Najibullah communist regime was able to resist the mujahideen for quite some time. Soviet foreign minister Eduard Shevardnadze traveled to Islamabad in the midst of the Red Army's departure to discuss a political compromise with Benazir. Although sympathetic to the idea, she confessed that the issue was in the hands of hard-liners in the ISI who opposed any settlement and assured him that Najibullah would soon fall. But Kabul did not crumble until much later.

Afghan commander Hekmatyar, solidly backed by the ISI, refused any type of compromise and obstinately demanded the presidency of Afghanistan. Ethnic rivalries reemerged, and soon enough, a brutal civil war erupted among the various factions of the mujahideen. The Taliban—young Pashtun refugees indoctrinated in madrassas in Pakistan's Balochistan Province who had multiplied under the Zia ul-Haq regime—emerged as a direct consequence of the rapid disintegration of the country and the reemerging rule of warlords.

But as Bush began his presidential term in January 1989, the United States had achieved its goal in Afghanistan. The Soviets had withdrawn, and two years later, the Soviet Union ceased to exist. Benazir's star power, along with intelligence reports that Pakistan had stopped producing weapons-grade uranium and Washington's desire to bolster the country's restored democracy, led Bush to grant the required certification and to confirm that the United States would sell Pakistan F-16 fighter jets and would continue military and economic aid to the tune of $600 million a year. The American-Pakistani relationship was back to normal.

Nevertheless, Robert Oakley, the American ambassador in

Islamabad who had a fluid dialogue with Benazir, warned the prime minister that Pakistan was about to commit political suicide unless it rolled back its nuclear capability. Sure enough, in October 1990 Bush refused to issue a certification under the Pressler Amendment.

Despite the warnings, Pakistani officials did not believe that the United States would actually implement the threat to cut aid. But without the certification, purchased F-16 fighters were not given an export license, and some frigates leased to the Pakistani navy on a no-cost basis had to be returned to the US Navy. General Beg voiced a widespread Pakistani opinion: the Afghan war was over and the Soviets had left; now the United States did not have to pretend any longer that the nuclear issue did not exist.

Benazir Bhutto was dismissed as prime minister by President Ghulam Ishaq and General Beg in November 1990, which tarnished Pakistan's image in the eyes of many influential American legislators. The caretaker government in Islamabad was careful to support the US military buildup in Saudi Arabia following Saddam Hussein's invasion of Kuwait in August 1990 that would lead to the Gulf War.

THE TERRORISM AND nuclear issues surfaced again when Nawaz Sharif replaced Benazir Bhutto as prime minister. The CIA warned the ISI of dire consequences if it continued to train and send Islamic extremists to combat Indians in Kashmir, including Arab veterans of the Afghan resistance. Sharif at least had to crack down on the Arab radicals in Pakistan.

Prime Minister Sharif named Lieutenant General Javed Nasir as ISI director general. A religious fundamentalist supporter, Nasir expanded ISI's activities worldwide, supporting Chinese Muslims in Xinjiang Province—instigating a protest from Beijing. Nasir also aided rebel Muslims in the Philippines and other radical religious outfits in Central Asia. The US State Department thus placed Pakistan on its terrorist states watch list, and in April 1993, the White House demanded that Javed Nasir be removed as head of the ISI. Sharif readily complied.

Bilateral relations improved after voters returned Benazir to the post of prime minister in 1993, with President Clinton in the White House. Following a policy initiated during the Bush administration, Clinton gave up on the idea of pushing for a rollback of the Pakistani nuclear program and instead settled for a freeze.

Benazir won positive points in Washington when, in early 1995, Pakistan arrested and then extradited Ramzi Yousef in an operation that incorporated American security officers. Yousef, an Islamic militant feared by Bhutto, had organized assassination attempts against her and stood accused of being the mastermind of the 1993 terrorist bombing of the World Trade Center in New York that killed six people and injured hundreds. During her April 1995 visit to Washington, Bhutto was once more favorably received by the media and political elite.

When the Afghans, fed up with the warlords' continued fighting and corruption, welcomed the Taliban, the Pakistani government saw a new opportunity to influence events in Afghanistan.

Naseerullah Babar, Benazir Bhutto's interior minister, ordered the ISI to provide logistical support and training for the Taliban (which means "students") movement that was expanding around Kandahar in the summer of 1994. The Taliban defeated Hekmatyar, the former favorite of the ISI, and the Pakistanis placed their bets on the Pashtuns, the tribal siblings of Pakistan's Pathans, to beat the other ethnic groups and capture the Afghan government. Kabul was taken on September 26, 1996.

Benazir Bhutto was dismissed, once again, as prime minister by a civilian president on accusations of mismanagement and charges of corruption against her and husband Asif Ali Zardari. Nawaz Sharif, who then returned to the post of prime minister after gaining a clear electoral victory, was keen to cooperate with Washington on the terrorism issue. In June 1997, he allowed a joint US-Pakistani police operation to capture Mir Aimal Kansi, a Pakistani charged with the 1993 killings of two CIA employees outside the agency's headquarters in Langley, Virginia, and to take Kansi to the United States without having to go through the customary extradition procedure.

The nuclear issue took center stage when the Hindu nationalist government of Atal Bihari Vajpayee in New Delhi detonated several nuclear devices on May 11, 1998, surprising Pakistan, the United States, and the world. Clinton imposed sanctions on India, cutting off all aid and voting against India in international financial institutions, while he tried arduously to convince Pakistan not to follow suit, promising, instead, a vigorous resumption of economic and military aid. But the political pressures facing Sharif were impossible to resist. On May 28, 1998, Pakistan detonated five underground nuclear devices and, on May 31, an additional one.

The US government strongly supported Indian-Pakistani talks in Lahore in early 1999 as a way to reduce tensions and advance a peace agenda. However, another ISI-supported insurgent operation in Kashmir involving the occupation of the highland town of Kargil, beyond the Line of Control, erupted into another bilateral crisis. New Delhi employed air power for the first time in Kashmir and advanced with a strong counterattack.

Nawaz Sharif called President Clinton and asked if he could come to Washington on July 4 to discuss the dangerous standoff with India. Sharif requested that Clinton use his good offices to resolve the crisis and, in addition, mediate with the Indians on Kashmir itself.

In his memoir, Clinton wrote that he told Nawaz Sharif that although it was Independence Day in the United States, he was willing to receive the Pakistani prime minister; but first, Sharif had to agree to withdraw the forces commanded by General Pervez Musharraf back across the Line of Control, and second, the US president would not intervene in the Kashmir dispute.[24] In Pakistan, General Musharraf felt that if Sharif went to Washington under those conditions, it was equivalent to capitulation. Sharif went to Washington anyway. Being a sharp politician, Clinton perceived that Sharif had traveled to Washington "in order to use pressure from the United States to provide himself cover for ordering his military to defuse the conflict."[25]

President Clinton agreed to help Sharif—not just to get him out of an unstable situation, but to force the prime minister to cooperate much more in the fight against terrorism. At that same July 4 meeting, the American president reminded Sharif that he had asked him on three occasions for help in apprehending Osama bin Laden. This time he told the prime minister that unless he was more forthcoming, he would have to announce that Pakistan was, in effect, supporting terrorism in Afghanistan.

As relations between Sharif and Musharraf deteriorated, the prime minister sent his brother Shahbaz Sharif to Washington DC in September to, once again, request US support to counter threats coming from the army due to the Pakistani withdrawal from Kargil. A couple of days later, a US government message to the Pakistani military read, "We hope there will be no return to days of interrupted democracy in Pakistan."[26] But as Clinton expected, Sharif did not last long and was overthrown by General Pervez Musharraf. The White House imposed additional sanctions on Pakistan, legally required in case of an overthrow of a democratically elected government.

In Afghanistan, the Taliban regime had become internationally isolated due to its treatment of women and children, its tolerance for drug trafficking, and its provision of safe haven for Islamic terrorists, including Osama bin Laden. The Americans had strong evidence that the terrorist attacks on the US embassies in Kenya and Tanzania in 1998, which took more than two hundred lives, had been organized by bin Laden, now living in Afghanistan under Taliban protection.

When American intelligence discovered that senior Al-Qaida recruiter Abu Zubaydah was operating openly from a house in Peshawar and sending foreign recruits to Afghanistan, US ambassador William Milam asked Musharraf to hand over Zubaydah, but the ISI responded that they could not find him, even though—the American ambassador asserted—"everyone knew where [Zubaydah] was."[27]

When President Clinton visited Islamabad in March 2000, he did so for only five hours, in contrast to the five days he spent in India. Clinton told Musharraf that he was prepared to help Indian-Pakistani talks on Kashmir and nonproliferation, but Islamabad had to rein in terrorist groups in Kashmir, pressure the Taliban to hand over bin Laden, and initiate peace talks. On the other key issue of democratic elections, Musharraf declined to provide a concrete timetable.

General Musharraf dismissed the American stand on terrorism. "The perceptions are different in the United States and in Pakistan, in the West and what we understand is terrorism," Musharraf declared shortly after Clinton's brief visit. He added that "Pakistan's strategic interests lay with supporting the Afghan Pashtuns," whom he associated solely with the Taliban.[28]

Pakistan's ISI even protected the Taliban acting on Pakistani territory, including the assassins of Abdul Ahad Karzai—the father of Hamid Karzai—shot dead in 1999 as he came out of a Quetta mosque. The Pakistani police never caught the assassins or the murderers of more than a dozen prominent Afghans opposed to the Taliban living in Pakistan.[29] Hamid Karzai himself was told by the ISI in 2001 that he could no longer stay in Pakistan and that his visa would not be renewed. The ISI—as analyst Ahmed Rashid put it—"was merely obliging the Taliban."[30]

THE GEORGE W. BUSH administration undertook a different approach with the Musharraf regime. Though Al-Qaida had struck again in October 2000, when suicide bombers rammed a swift boat packed with explosives into the USS *Cole*, an American destroyer anchored at Aden harbor, killing seventeen US sailors and wounding many others, Deputy Secretary Armitage declared that Washington did "not want to see Pakistan only through the lens of Osama bin Laden"[31] and did not wish to witness Pakistan follow the path of Afghanistan and become a failed state. But 9/11 changed all that, forcing the US-Pakistani relationship to become a partnership centered on the Taliban–Al-Qaida threat and the war on terror.

In anticipation of the US attack against the Taliban, bin Laden escaped his home in Kandahar, and some of his top lieutenants moved out of Afghanistan. To avoid putting boots on the ground, the Americans coupled air bombings with support for the Afghan Northern Alliance forces led by Ahmad Shah Massoud. The CIA had no contacts among the Pashtuns in the south and had to rely on the ISI.

As the American air strikes continued, ISI officers helped American colleagues locate Taliban targets for US bombers, while at the same time, "other ISI officers were pumping fresh armaments to the Taliban."[32] Musharraf took these contradictory steps because an overthrow of the Taliban would not only eliminate an ally of Islamabad in its "strategic depth" policy but also potentially lead to a pro-Indian regime in Kabul.

Kabul fell in mid-November 2001 to Northern Alliance troops. The Taliban, after looting the capital, fled toward the south. That was ISI territory, and US authorities instructed the CIA to do nothing without consulting the ISI. Finally, the Taliban were surrounded by Northern Alliance forces, and in the city of Kunduz, hundreds of ISI officers who had fought along with the Taliban were caught in the cross fire, unable to escape. Musharraf phoned President Bush and requested a pause in the bombing and the opening of a corridor so that Pakistani aircraft could evacuate his officers out of Kunduz. Vice President Dick Cheney took charge, and both he and Bush said yes to Musharraf, approving a top-secret evacuation operation without the knowledge of Secretary of State Colin Powell. Reports indicated that along with the ISI officers, many Taliban and Al-Qaida leaders escaped in the airlift operation.[33] Learned observers estimate that more foreign terrorists escaped from Kunduz than the six hundred or so previously reported, including Osama bin Laden, who slipped out later from Tora Bora, escorted by Pashtun guides from the Pakistani side of the border, to relocate in Pakistan's South and North Waziristan.

On December 13, 2001, Hamid Karzai boarded a US military plane in Kandahar bound for Kabul to take over as president. He had just declined an offer from Musharraf to travel via Islamabad. For Pakistan, the configuration of the new government in Kabul was a disaster. Islamabad would shun Karzai and continue to help the escaping Taliban. In contrast, India strongly supported Karzai, set up a sizable diplomatic presence in Kabul, and established cooperation programs.

Musharraf began to play a delicate double game. He helped the American war effort, but he did not abandon the Taliban. World reality had changed, but he could not overlook domestic pressures and Pakistan's long-term interests in Kabul. US authorities detected Pakistan's assistance to the Taliban, but, initially, they were unsure of how high up it went in Islamabad.

In early 2002, India-Pakistan tensions rose to a dangerous level in the wake of bombings in Kashmir and an attack by Pakistani-based militants against the Indian Parliament. Bush gave an ultimatum to Musharraf to crack down on terror and make an unequivocal public statement on the subject. Musharraf delivered a speech on January 12—in which American diplomats in Islamabad had significant input—where for the first time he spoke against jihad and announced the banning of five extremist groups, followed by the arrests of hundreds of militants.

The nuclear issue came back on the bilateral agenda in new form—this time linked to terrorism, as the CIA asked the ISI to arrest two retired Pakistani nuclear scientists (who were also Al-Qaida militants) who had been in touch with Osama bin Laden around 9/11 as well as with active nuclear scientists. The CIA's chief, George Tenet, secretly traveled to Islamabad to ask that Musharraf allow the CIA to interrogate the scientists and, moreover, to request that the general conduct an extensive purge of ISI officers suspected of being close to terrorists.

The Musharraf government implemented a clever strategy of capturing escaping Al-Qaida leaders to hand them over and satisfy the Americans. Abu Zubaydah, a top Al-Qaida leader, was captured in Faisalabad; then, Ramzi bin al-Shibh, one of the leaders of the Hamburg cell that planned 9/11, was caught in Karachi. Cheney argued within the Bush administration that these coups demonstrated that Musharraf should not be criticized in other areas, such as the restoration of democratic rule. The administration did not consider the return of civilian politicians like Bhutto to be an indispensable priority.

In February 2002, Musharraf visited President Bush at the White House—an event characterized by abundant handshakes, smiles, posed photographs, and compliments. Bush, in line with his personal approach to diplomacy, declared, "When [Musharraf] looks me in the eye and says there won't be a Taliban and won't be Al-Qaida, I believe him, you know?"[34] Bush had called the general "my buddy," and during this White House visit, he stated that he was proud to call Musharraf a friend. The American president also applauded what he portrayed as Musharraf's vision of "Pakistan as a progressive, modern and democratic Islamic society."[35]

The visit was positive for Musharraf. Although he did not get the trade concessions he sought, Bush announced a package of increased economic and military aid. Musharraf's warm reception in Washington helped him to "demonstrate to his home audience that his decision to side with the United States had paid off."[36]

But the visit did not completely distract from the terrorist problem. Musharraf's sojourn to Washington coincided with the disappearance of Daniel Pearl, the American reporter for the *Wall Street Journal*, which ended in his gruesome murder by terrorist Ahmed Omar Sheikh. When discovered, Omar Sheikh gave himself up to a former ISI officer, Brigadier General Ijaz Shah, who was home secretary of Punjab Province at the time. The police were informed of Sheikh's surrender one full week after he was under the care of the former ISI officer.[37] Islamabad refused Washington's request to extradite Omar Sheikh to the United States.

Not long after, toward the end of that same year, the Bush-Musharraf honeymoon was facing trouble. American intelligence had detected "the world's largest concentration of Al Qaida operatives" in Pakistan and Afghanistan and discovered that Al-Qaida operatives were finding "refuge in Pakistan and starting to regroup and move back into Afghanistan."[38] Moreover, National Security Adviser Condoleezza Rice took a public swipe at Musharraf during his third visit to the United States in October 2002, declaring that the White House objected to some actions taken by the general, including his twenty-nine arbitrary amendments to the constitution; she warned that the United States would not "compromise in terms of democratic principles"[39] and would not entirely look the other way on human rights. Musharraf continued to pursue a double policy of cooperation and conflict with the United States. More Al-Qaida leaders were captured, including Khalid Sheikh Mohammed. But the Americans detected a parallel and clandestine ISI network being constituted by retired intelligence officials and former trainers of the Taliban, who set up offices in Peshawar, Quetta, and other Pakistani cities to run training camps for the Taliban with arms and funds coming from the Gulf countries.[40] ISI's Section S, in charge of external operations, was providing the Afghan insurgents with sanctuary, money, and logistical support. Moreover, ISI agents maintained regular contact with fugitive Mullah Omar, Jalaluddin Haqqani, and other militants. In addition, Musharraf had legitimized extremists by allowing banned groups to organize conferences and denying the Al-Qaida links with the Jamaat-e-Islami party—which had bitterly opposed and undermined Benazir Bhutto's government.

Meanwhile, President Karzai complained that no senior American would criticize Musharraf for allowing the Taliban to operate freely in Pakistan. On a visit to Islamabad, Karzai had given Musharraf a list of Taliban commanders supposedly living openly in Quetta.[41] But Musharraf felt no sympathy for the Karzai regime and its growing friendship with India. Meanwhile, the Americans were more worried about Al-Qaida than about the Taliban.

Musharraf's double game angered both sides. The Taliban and Al-Qaida felt betrayed by the arrests and banning of extremist religious parties and reacted with violence against their protectors and creators, attacking the Pakistani army and even attempting to kill Musharraf.

General Musharraf was the target of two assassination attempts in December 2003. After the first attack, on December 14, he ordered Lieutenant General Ashfaq Parvez Kayani, at the time Rawalpindi corps commander, to lead the investigation. An explosive charge activated by a cell phone call had narrowly missed General Musharraf's three-ton Mercedes as it crossed a bridge in Rawalpindi, but it had left valuable forensic leads. Diligent investigators found a small piece of a cell phone keypad that eventually led to the culprits. After the second assassination attempt, the investigators sealed off the area of the attack, and immediately ISI, MI, and police personnel were on the scene collecting forensic evidence. They discovered the blown-off face of an individual, a half-burned ID card, and the remains of a cell phone on the roof of a nearby building. According to Musharraf, "a meticulous search of the area helped to find the SIM card. Surprisingly it was intact."[42] These clues and further investigation led to the arrest of the attackers. These thorough investigations stood in stark contrast with what happened after Benazir Bhutto's assassination.

The White House did not like the ambivalent Pakistani attitude in the war on terror, but it was patient, believing that pushing Musharraf too hard would be counterproductive. Led by Vice

President Dick Cheney, the US government believed that Musharraf was the best option available in the strategy to fight Al-Qaida. In 2004, demonstrating that the White House still had faith in Musharraf, Bush conferred the status of "non-NATO ally" on Pakistan and approved a $700 million aid package.

The US government became increasingly impatient with the lack of Pakistani progress in the fight against the militants and launched episodic missile strikes against Al-Qaida targets in North and South Waziristan. A controversial accord signed in September 2006 by Islamabad and a group of Pakistani Taliban leaders in North Waziristan—which sought to stop all attacks on American and Afghan forces in Afghanistan and on the Pakistani army in return for Islamabad's withdrawal of its garrisons and checkpoints and the release of prisoners and captured equipment—produced a cessation of attacks on American troops in Afghanistan. The Bush administration, which welcomed the deal at first, declared it a failure three months after its signing when it became clear that the tribal areas were increasingly the point of origin of Al-Qaida terrorist plots around the world.

Washington's displeasure with Musharraf also included the discovery that A. Q. Khan had been engaged in nuclear proliferation activities with North Korea, Libya, and Iran. A. Q. Khan confessed publicly and was placed under house arrest. Bush did not want to push the case any further so as not to provoke a nationalist reaction that could endanger Islamabad's support in the war on terror.[43]

IN 2007, AS Musharraf's Pakistan faced growing instability and political strain within and without, the United States came to see the presence of Benazir Bhutto as more and more important. Musharraf's dismissal of Chief Justice Iftikhar Muhammad Chaudhry had generated public debates, rallies, and street demonstrations calling for his reinstatement. This opposition soon became known as the "Lawyers' movement," growing over the course of the year into one of the largest mass movements in Pakistan's history. It galvanized a broad range of sentiments opposed to continued military rule. In parallel, there was a steep increase in extremist violence by radical Islamists, especially after the government's attack on pro-Taliban militants and their supporters who had occupied the Red Mosque, in the heart of Islamabad, which led to a weeklong battle. Official figures indicate that forty-four suicide bombings took place in 2007, killing 614 people—a dramatic rise from eight such incidents in 2006.

Preparing for new parliamentary elections and the electoral college vote for the presidency, Pakistan's two main opposition political parties, Benazir Bhutto's PPP and the PML-N, put aside their long-term rivalry and worked together to define a common framework for a return to democratic rule. This agreement, the Charter of Democracy, was signed in May 2006 by Benazir Bhutto and Nawaz Sharif, the respective leaders of the PPP and the PML-N.

Bhutto understood that if she were to return to Pakistan to lead the fight for democracy and for her own vindication as a political figure, she would need to engage in a difficult rapprochement with General Musharraf. Fortunately for her, the United States and the United Kingdom were losing faith in Musharraf.

The idea that Musharraf was the only person capable of holding Pakistan together and keeping the army in the fight against terrorists began to erode. First, he wasn't being efficient in fighting terror. Extremist activities and nuclear proliferation were making Pakistan the "most dangerous place in the world," as former secretary of state Madeleine K. Albright would characterize the country some time later.[44] Dick Cheney grew more isolated in his defense of Musharraf as US army officers complained about the uneven playing field in Afghanistan, given the Pakistani-permitted Taliban sanctuaries in the tribal regions. Second, the general's lack of democratic legitimacy was becoming a larger domestic problem.

Washington believed that a political adjustment was needed. "Musharraf was on borrowed time in Pakistan," wrote the then US secretary of state Condoleezza Rice in her memoir. The answer, according to Rice, "lay in forging an alliance between the two strongest political forces in the country: Musharraf and former Prime Minister Benazir Bhutto."[45] Musharraf had to keep the military in line, but Benazir Bhutto had to be brought on board to provide democratic legitimacy to a broader coalition government and a more committed stand on terrorism with wider domestic political backing.

Benazir Bhutto descending from a plane at Karachi airport and waving to supporters upon arrival back in her homeland on October 18, 2007, following years of self-imposed exile, accompanied by advisers and leading members of her party. The US and UK governments were key facilitators of her return to Pakistan.

6

The US-Brokered Return of Bhutto to Her Homeland

On June 20, 2004, Benazir Bhutto was attending a dinner in Blackburn, England, a Lancashire town with a significant Pakistani population historically sympathetic to Bhutto. Her host was Salas Kiani, a British Pakistani who had served as the town's mayor. During the meal, Kiani received a call on his mobile phone and handed it to a surprised Benazir: "It's Jack—for you," said Kiani mischievously. Foreign Secretary Jack Straw, an MP for Blackburn, was on the line; years earlier, Straw, then home secretary, had refused to receive Bhutto after she had been deposed as prime minister, but now he invited her to visit him at the Foreign Office. This was the first communication the PPP leader had had with a British minister in more than a decade.[1]

One morning the following month, Bhutto was brought into the Foreign Office through a discreet side entrance. The last time she had met with a top British official had been in 1995 when Tony Blair, a friend of Bhutto's since their time at Oxford, had attended a dinner hosted by her and husband Asif Ali Zardari at the Savoy. At the encounter with Straw, which lasted one hour, the foreign secretary assured Benazir that London favored democracy for Pakistan, but he stressed that Musharraf had to be part of the picture. From then on, the UK government through the British high commissioner in Islamabad, Mark Lyall Grant, began to convey messages to Benazir from Musharraf about the initial terms of a negotiation: Musharraf would not retire from the army until after his parliamentary election as president, and Benazir would benefit from a legal ruling withdrawing all corruption cases pending against her and other opposition politicians.

Mutual distrust and disagreement had impeded concrete progress in past conversations. In 2002, according to Benazir, ISI officials had proposed by phone that if the former prime minister stayed out of politics for ten years, they would release her husband from jail. But this time, Musharraf offered to release her husband as a gesture of goodwill, which he did in November 2004.

New talks between Bhutto and Straw followed at the Foreign Office in 2005, where London expressed apprehension about chaos in Pakistan and championed the need to ensure a smooth, sustainable transition to democracy. Straw was now working with US secretary of state Condoleezza Rice, who believed that Washington had to play a more active role to enable a stable post-Musharraf scenario in Pakistan.

At the time, the White House still believed that Musharraf was the best hope for stopping Islamic extremists in Pakistan. Vice President Dick Cheney, in particular, was not willing to break the "Mush-Bush axis," as Pakistani journalists called the bilateral relationship. Yet despite Cheney's trust, the general was not stopping the militants. Some in Washington suspected Musharraf was trying to please everyone, including the militants and their religious supporters. The US administration grew interested in opening channels for an eventual political agreement between the two leaders. Bhutto could provide her political party base and democratic credentials as well as closeness to the West. The White House also knew that Bhutto could not return to Pakistan unless Musharraf eliminated the judicial charges pending against her.

Some of Musharraf's closest advisers also encouraged him to open channels with Bhutto, thinking such an alliance could shore up political support for his next presidential term. A discreet process was set in motion. Benazir was the first to reach out to the Musharraf government through security adviser Rehman Malik. At least five meetings followed in 2005 and 2006 between her and Musharraf's team, which included Tariq Aziz, former secretary of the National Security Council; General Ashfaq Parvez Kayani, then director general of the ISI; and, in later meetings, Lieutenant General Hamid Javed, Musharraf's chief of staff. Bhutto and Musharraf never met face-to-face during that period.

The governments of the United Kingdom and the United States actively facilitated the talks between the two leaders. Both governments prioritized a continued leadership role for General Musharraf, as they believed this was vital for the ongoing war on terror. Washington was particularly interested in achieving a degree of political stability in Pakistan that would enable the government to more effectively confront domestic militancy. At the same time, Washington and London believed both efforts could be strengthened with a credible civilian partner. Since Musharraf and Nawaz Sharif, in exile in Saudi Arabia, disliked each other intensely, Bhutto was the only option. It was hoped that the talks could yield some formula for a power-sharing deal.

While these meetings were important for identifying areas of common interest, they did not produce any concrete agreements. Little progress was made. In August 2006, while Bhutto was in New York, General Musharraf phoned to ask for her support for a bill promoting women's rights. He also stressed that moderate forces should work together. Benazir agreed. But Benazir insisted on a detailed road map to democracy. Musharraf wanted Benazir to opt out of the next general election. With the failure of each round of talks, relations between the two camps soured.

TO BREAK THE stalemate, a direct meeting between Bhutto and Musharraf was arranged, and the two met secretly on January 24, 2007, in Abu Dhabi. Benazir was flown by helicopter to the green gardens of the palace of Sheikh Zayed bin Sultan Al Nahyan, where a long and positive discussion took place. According to Benazir, Musharraf agreed to retire from the army before the national elections and offered, as a confidence-building measure, to terminate the judicial cases against her and her husband Asif. In turn, Bhutto agreed not to return to Pakistan before December 31, 2007.[2] Musharraf told Benazir that for her own security she should not come back until after the elections, scheduled for January 8, 2008, because militants were likely to attack her. Benazir, along with a few close advisers, including Rehman Malik and Makhdoom Amin Fahim, would follow up with Musharraf's team in the coming months.

Former secretary of state Condoleezza Rice wrote in her memoir *No Higher Honor* that the United States was actively involved in the negotiations between Musharraf and Bhutto, with particular intensity during the spring and summer of 2007. As early as 2006, according to an ISI source, the United States believed that Musharraf was becoming an increasing political liability and began to advise him to take a course of political reconciliation with Bhutto.

Richard Boucher, the assistant secretary for South and Central Asian affairs, became the point man for the US mediation effort, as stated by former secretary Rice in her memoir and confirmed by our UN commission. Boucher shuttled back and forth between the two leaders and their top advisers, meeting them in London or Dubai.

In early 2007, President George W. Bush made his first public criticism of Musharraf, warning that he had to be more aggressive in pursuing the terrorists. Secretary Rice intensified her direct engagement with the two sides, attempting to bridge the differences.

After his January 2007 meeting with Bhutto, General Musharraf began informing his close political allies, including PML-Q leadership, about the process. Many of them expressed deep reservations. They argued against seeking Bhutto's PPP support for Musharraf's reelection, confident that they could win the presidency and parliamentary elections alone and concerned that a broadened alliance would diminish their power. Similarly, few in the PPP senior leadership believed that an alliance with Musharraf would benefit the party. Suspicion lingered particularly when Musharraf made an anomalous proposal: if Benazir stayed away from Pakistan during the election, "Musharraf would adjust the vote" to give the PPP more seats than they might otherwise get.[3] In other words, Musharraf was suggesting he might rig the election, by consensus.

Despite the doubts in the PPP camp, Benazir was open to a deal. According to close friends and advisers, Benazir had matured politically since she was prime minister in the late '90s; she was less impatient, more thoughtful and focused, and knew that politics required vision, pragmatism, and leadership, even against the tide of public opinion and her own party.

That spring, Benazir spoke publicly about her disposition to craft an agreement with Musharraf. She told the *Sunday Times* in April 2007, "I want a deal with President Musharraf, but it would be premature to say one is imminent."[4] To create a favorable atmosphere for the deal, Benazir praised Musharraf for protecting minorities and women, although she blamed the general for the growing influence of the Taliban in Waziristan that had forced Musharraf to negotiate a peace accord with them. In that interview, she vowed to return to Pakistan despite "the danger of assassination by Islamists," whom she accused of bringing the Taliban to Islamabad.

Benazir and General Musharraf met again face-to-face in Abu Dhabi in July 2007, in the wake of Musharraf's confrontation with the chief justice of the Supreme Court and the Red Mosque armed conflict. The general raised the issue of reducing the age of retirement for members of the superior judiciary, to which Benazir responded negatively. Musharraf asserted that the judicial cases against her and husband Asif could not be dismissed. Benazir then asked that Musharraf at least lift the ban on twice-elected prime ministers, and Musharraf agreed. Again, Musharraf insisted that she not come back until after the elections; he said the intelligence agencies were intercepting a growing number of security threats on the hundreds of phone lines they monitored. Benazir took seriously the threats conveyed by the government, but believed Musharraf used them as a ploy to keep her away from campaigning in Pakistan, particularly in view that her desperate calls for security assistance to respond to those threats went unheard.

As recounted to the commission by interlocutors from all parties, Bhutto laid out several issues of concern in the negotiations. The most important of these were the following: (1) her return to Pakistan to participate in politics; (2) free and fair elections in 2007; (3) Musharraf's resignation from the army; (4)

amnesty in the criminal cases against her and her husband; and (5) the elimination of the ban on third terms for former prime ministers, which was impeding her from holding office again. The same sources indicated that Musharraf's chief goals were to ensure his continuity in power by accommodating US and other international desire for Bhutto's return.

MEDIA COVERAGE OF the process led to a generalized perception that they would likely govern together after the elections, with Musharraf continuing as president and Bhutto serving as prime minister. A number of sources interviewed by the commission confirmed that this option had been under discussion, but many said that the outcome depended on the results of the general elections. At some point, Benazir suggested to Musharraf that if she became prime minister, he could remain as president and occupy the posts of minister of defense and minister of foreign affairs, but Musharraf dismissed the idea as "unconstitutional."

A significant problem was that the PML-Q leadership had also been assured by Musharraf that if they won the elections, their leader Chaudhry Pervaiz Elahi would become the next prime minister. Other options, such as Bhutto becoming Senate chairperson, had also been raised. The specific terms of a power-sharing agreement between Bhutto and Musharraf were fluid and never unequivocally finalized.

In August and September 2007, there were intense behind-the-scenes discussions between Bhutto and Musharraf and their respective teams with US facilitation. In her three-week visit to the United States in August, Benazir met with her PPP leadership in New York to prepare a document on what they expected from Musharraf's side, and again met with Assistant Secretary Boucher and with her friend Zalmay Khalilzad, the former US ambassador to Afghanistan. These conversations convinced her that Washington would put serious pressure on Musharraf to agree to a deal.

Both Bhutto and Musharraf shared an increasing sense of urgency but had different priorities. For Bhutto, the most pressing concern was the creation of a legal mechanism to eliminate old criminal corruption charges leveled against her and her husband; for Musharraf, the most immediate issue was ensuring PPP support for his reelection as president. After other meetings in London and Islamabad and many last-minute discussions, compromise agreements on both core issues were reached in the first week of October, less than two weeks before Bhutto's announced return.

The tentative deal, according to former secretary Rice, who had spoken and negotiated with both parties on October 3, 2007, was "not firm but detailed enough that Bhutto would be permitted to return to Pakistan to stand in the parliamentary elections that would be held by mid-January."[5] Rice added that the deal had been complicated by rumors that Musharraf would take off his uniform only after the elections and that, therefore, he would stand for elections as army chief. Rice recounted that Benazir thought that there was a "U.S. guarantee" that he would do so.[6]

Negotiations on the issue of the old criminal cases were turned over to high-level representatives of the PML-Q and PPP, who met at least twice in September at an ISI safe house in Islamabad. During these and later meetings, they drafted what would become the National Reconciliation Ordinance (NRO), which provided a virtual amnesty for political figures "found to have been falsely involved for political reasons or through political victimization in cases" brought against them between 1986 and October 1999. On October 5, 2007, Musharraf signed the NRO. On October 6, he was reelected president by the electoral college, composed of the members of the sitting Parliament and Provincial Assemblies. Bhutto had agreed that although the PPP members would abstain from the vote, they would stay in the session, thus allowing for the required quorum after other opposition party members refused to participate and withdrew. This enabled the PML-Q vote in favor of Musharraf, equivalent to 57 percent of the total number of MPs, to carry the day.

According to several sources, Musharraf was unable to convince the PML-Q to agree to support the lifting of the ban on third terms. Party leaders were deeply opposed to the measure, as they feared it would ultimately diminish their power, facilitate Nawaz Sharif's return, and give a boost in the elections to both Bhutto and Sharif. Thus, there was never any agreement to create the legal possibility of a third term for Bhutto.

This situation made it all the more important to Bhutto that the elections be conducted in a free and fair manner. In addition to the history of ISI vote rigging in previous elections, there were well-documented problems with the 2007 voter lists, which had to be redone at midyear, along with thousands of complaints from PPP and PML-N activists that PML-Q authorities were preparing the ground for local rigging. In fact, after the July meeting between Benazir and Musharraf in Abu Dhabi, she had secretly sent an aide to Islamabad to review the work of the firm hired to create a new electoral list. The aide's site visits for this purpose were facilitated directly by ISI chief General Kayani and other ISI officers. General Kayani had assured Bhutto's people that in 2007 there would be no rigging. For Benazir to become prime minister, the PPP would have to win the elections with a sufficient majority and build the needed alliances to ensure that, in a new National Assembly, they could pass legislation allowing a third term. This placed additional pressure on her, not only to be vigilant on potential rigging but also to carry out a vigorous public campaign to win votes for herself and her party more broadly.

General Musharraf became very unhappy when Bhutto announced a pre-election return date. No agreement was ever reached on this issue, or on a complete deal, as Musharraf said in an interview we had with him in October 2009. The general did not want Benazir to return to Pakistan until after the election campaign was over. "Come on December 31st and then we can celebrate the New Year together," Musharraf had allegedly told Bhutto in one of their last conversations. "Two hundred percent she was not supposed to come back when she did," Musharraf responded to one of my questions. But Bhutto knew she needed to campaign for herself and the PPP for the January 8 elections. She picked October 18 as the day of her homecoming.

After she announced the date she would return to Pakistan, Bhutto began, around September 2007, to raise concerns regarding personal security, especially in her communications with American officials. US government representatives told the commission that they provided advice to Bhutto on hiring Pakistani private security firms used by diplomatic missions and spoke at least once with the Musharraf camp about her security arrangements. The same officials noted, however, that the United States had not accepted any responsibility for Bhutto's security in Pakistan. A cable—revealed by WikiLeaks—from the US embassy in Islamabad to Washington, dated October 27 and signed by Ambassador Anne W. Patterson, stated that, indeed, the embassy provided names of security contractors with knowledge of the indigenous environment and political culture to Benazir's advisers. It further related that, on the same day, the ambassador had met with Musharraf's national security adviser Tariq Aziz to reiterate "the government's responsibility for Bhutto's security."[7]

Upon being contacted by some of Benazir's American advisers, representatives of the security firm Blackwater flew to Dubai to offer her several security options, costing an average of $400,000 monthly. Since Musharraf had opposed the idea of foreign security forces accompanying Benazir on her return to Pakistan, Blackwater intended to work with affiliated contractors in the country. But Benazir rejected this option.[8] Sources close to her told our commission that she preferred the United States to urge Musharraf to provide her with all necessary security. A high-placed source in the US government I consulted assured me that Benazir was upset that the United States had been unwilling or unable to persuade Musharraf from denying her the use of armed security on the basis of legal impediments.

According to senior journalist and writer Ron Suskind, who accompanied Benazir Bhutto to several meetings before and after her return to Pakistan, she was so concerned about her security that she went to the US Congress to speak with key members like Senator John Kerry to request assistance. Kerry offered to speak to the State Department, which had already received assurances from Musharraf that he would provide Bhutto enough security. But knowing the realities of power in Washington, she insisted to her US interlocutors that Vice President Cheney be the one to call Musharraf to hold him responsible for her security. Cheney "is the only one that Musharraf will respect,"[9] she commented. But Cheney had only reluctantly gone along with the State Department–led plan to pressure Benazir into a political cohabitation arrangement with the general, and even then he felt the only purpose should be to lend legitimacy and support to Musharraf in the confrontation with militants, which he felt was top priority. Cheney wanted to reserve putting pressure on Musharraf for when they needed leverage to reinforce Islamabad's fight against terrorism.

Benazir's security concerns soon heightened in light of intelligence, communicated to her by United Arab Emirates officials but already known to the ISI, that extremists were planning to assassinate her. With Musharraf's government having rejected the idea of foreign security personnel, the general nominated two potential chief protection officers, both from the police, and Benazir chose Major Imtiaz, who had worked with her when she was prime minister. Benazir also picked her own drivers. Security adviser Rehman Malik ordered a specially armored Toyota Land Cruiser with a B6 level of protection. Guard dogs were bought for her residence, but, as they were not properly trained, were more a menace than a help and would indiscriminately attack anyone. According to several people close to Benazir whom we interviewed during the course of our investigation, she felt let down by the United States for not pushing Musharraf to improve her security; she also believed that the United States and the United Kingdom should have guaranteed her security, as her return was organized in close coordination with the UK and US governments.

Washington and London were the key external players advocating Bhutto's return to Pakistan, but they were not willing to assume responsibility for her security. In September 2007 Benazir sent an email to UK Foreign Secretary David Milliband naming the three individuals identified in her letter to Musharraf that she feared would try to do her harm. She hoped that Milliband would use his influence with Musharraf to remove those individuals from powerful positions from which they could plot against her.[10] During our investigation we held a constructive meeting with officials of the Foreign Office in London, when we asked about what measures the UK government had taken to ensure Benazir's safe return to Pakistan. We were promised detailed answers but we never received them, despite repeated reminders on our part.

AFTER THE TERRORIST attack in Karachi that killed dozens of her supporters and marred her return to Pakistan, a mutual "trust deficit" developed between Benazir and Musharraf. Although they managed to reestablish some discussions, their relationship essentially disintegrated when General Musharraf decided to declare emergency rule on November 3, 2007, suspend the constitution, promulgate a series of measures that amounted to martial law, and again sack Chief Justice Chaudhry, together with a number of other high court justices. The chief justice and two-thirds of the country's senior judges were put under house arrest. Musharraf explained the decision as necessary to contain the mounting extremist violence. But a former official of the Musharraf government told our commission that the general had considered declaring an emergency and suspending the constitution two months earlier and that the White House, upon learning of the plan, strongly advised against it and convinced Musharraf to backtrack. Now, in November, he was acting preemptively. He suspected that the Supreme Court would rule negatively on the legality of his recent reelection as president and his eligibility to hold dual posts as president and chief of army staff.

The PPP and PML-N launched political protests through the country against the emergency rule measures and against military rule. Bhutto announced the holding of a "long march" from Lahore to Islamabad. Violent clashes between police and protesters broke out in several cities. American diplomats asked Bhutto to restrain her criticisms of Musharraf. In November alone, the government acknowledged the arrest of some five thousand protesters; PPP and PML-N candidates were among them. Some in the PML-Q began to call for a postponement of the elections, adding an additional degree of uncertainty to the situation.

On November 9, Bhutto was briefly placed under house arrest. The next day, before domestic and international media, she broke ties with General Musharraf, denouncing his actions, calling for an end to the military government, and announcing that any deal with him was off.

Two motivations drove this decision. The first was simply to demonstrate her strong dissent toward the declaration of emergency. The second was more sophisticated. She increasingly realized that governing together with Musharraf would expose her to the growing public ire against his government. She feared that an ongoing political relationship with the general would weaken her politically, diminish her legitimacy, and lessen possibilities for a solid PPP electoral victory.

US Senator Joe Biden, then chairman of the Senate Foreign Relations Committee, called Benazir to assure her that the United States strongly favored lifting the emergency rule and setting a date for elections. In September, Deputy Secretary of State John D. Negroponte delivered that same message directly to Musharraf in Islamabad.[11] On November 16, 2007, Negroponte phoned Benazir to press in favor of resuming dialogue with Musharraf to put the democratic transition back on track.

Benazir complained to journalist and writer Ahmed Rashid that Vice President Cheney was putting all the pressure on her to "conform," while no similar pressure was being placed on Musharraf to show flexibility to achieve a bargain.[12] President Bush, according to Condoleezza Rice, didn't want "anyone pulling the rug" out from under Musharraf.[13] In Cheney's view, Musharraf needed to be defended as an essential player in the war against terror. Aware of her limited leverage with her American patrons, Benazir toned down her criticisms of Musharraf, although the general continued making abrasive comments about her.

Benazir was concerned that Musharraf could manipulate the dialogue process without making any concessions and that the ISI was preparing to rig the elections—as the US embassy in Islamabad was already reporting to Washington. She eventually reestablished communication with Musharraf through intermediaries but turned more of her energy toward the campaign and strengthening her relationship with Nawaz Sharif, who had been deposed as prime minister by General Musharraf in 1999, and Sharif's PML-N party. On November 25, Sharif was allowed to return to Pakistan from Saudi Arabia, following a failed attempt in September when he was detained at the airport and deported for violating the terms of the agreement that had sent him into exile ten years earlier. The PPP and the PML-N continued to discuss strategies for the elections and in some districts decided to run a single candidate.

The government confirmed that elections would go ahead on January 8, 2008, and Musharraf finally retired as army chief. He announced the lifting of emergency rule measures on December 16. Bhutto was assassinated eleven days later. By the time of her murder, the possibility of rehabilitating the relationship between the two had clearly waned. Neither Bhutto nor Musharraf believed that either of them still needed the support of the other to achieve their ultimate political goals.

A survivor stands amid the carnage of dead and wounded immediately following the bomb and gunfire attack that killed Benazir Bhutto at Liaquat Bagh, Rawalpindi, on December 27, 2007, following an electoral rally.

7

The Assassination

THE NIGHT BEFORE her assassination, Benazir Bhutto arrived in Islamabad to stay at Zardari House, her family's residence in the capital, after traveling by car from the city of Peshawar. Benazir was tired, but the director general of the ISI, Major General Nadeem Taj, had requested an urgent conversation with her. The former prime minister decided that she would sleep for a couple of hours and then receive the ISI chief at her house, in the early hours of December 27. The meeting took place around 1:30 a.m. Security adviser Rehman Malik accompanied Benazir during part of the conversation.

Major General Taj told Bhutto that the intelligence agency was concerned about a possible terrorist attack against her and urged Bhutto to limit her public exposure and keep a low profile at the campaign rally at Liaquat Bagh later that day. Intelligence officers from Saudi Arabia and the United Arab Emirates had arrived by private plane in Pakistan the day before, General Taj said, to convey credible information about a possible attack, which coincided with the revelation of ISI intelligence regarding a terrorist cell in Mardan that might attack her in Rawalpindi. Using communication-interception technology, the ISI had been tracking three separate Pakistani Taliban cells that were supposedly planning to attack Benazir, and the agency already knew about the information coming from the foreign intelligence counterparts. According to the ISI information, the terrorists involved in the operation had been instructed to shave their beards and change their traditional style of clothing so as not to attract attention.

Benazir did not lend much credence to the threats and told the ISI director general that evidently the government and the ISI did not want her "to do politics." Instead, she argued that the ISI should ensure that she would have proper protection and that her rally would be safe. She agreed, though, to minimize her exposure at the public event.

Much of the conversation with Nadeem Taj was about the coming elections. Benazir said that she hoped the ISI would not rig the elections against her. Taj responded that General Kayani's policy was that the ISI, from now on, was going to stay out of politics.

On that morning of December 27, Benazir Bhutto got up around 8:30 a.m. and had breakfast around 9:00. About an hour and a half later, Bhutto left, accompanied by Amin Fahim and a former PPP senator, to meet Afghan president Hamid Karzai at a fourth-floor suite in the capital's Serena Hotel. She returned about 1:30 p.m. to the Zardari House, where she had a light lunch and went over her speech for the Liaquat Bagh rally with a few close advisers. Witnesses recalled that she was upbeat because her dialogue with President Karzai had been positive. Bhutto was confident that she would be able to improve the relationship between Islamabad and Kabul and that together they could bring the unstable situation in the tribal areas under control. According to Karzai, she had also criticized the ISI for trying to undermine her.[1] The Afghan president, who had not met Benazir personally until then, was very impressed by the woman's courage; she seemed "too courageous for her own good," Karzai told a senior journalist.[2]

Before leaving the Zardari House at around 2:00 p.m., she asked Brigadier Aman, her private secretary, to slot two appointments for the rest of the day: one in the afternoon, with a European Union election observation mission, and the other that evening, with US Senator Arlen Specter and US Congressman Patrick Kennedy.

Benazir departed for Liaquat Bagh in a convoy of vehicles. The convoy was made up of a black Toyota Land Cruiser occupied by PPP security head Tauqir Kaira, followed by Bhutto's white armored Land Cruiser and two of Kaira's vehicles on either side of her vehicle. The latter two were a Mercedes-Benz van on the right and a four-door double-cab vehicle on the left. Immediately behind those vehicles were two Toyota Vigo pickup trucks from the Zardari House, positioned side by side. Behind these Vigos was a black Mercedes-Benz, from the Zardari House, which was bulletproof and served as the backup vehicle for Bhutto.

Security chief Tauqir Kaira was inside the lead vehicle with his men. Joining the former prime minister in her vehicle were Javed-ur-Rehman, the driver, who was seated in the front left seat; senior superintendent of police Major (ret.) Imtiaz Hussain, seated in the front right seat; Makhdoom Amin Fahim, senior PPP member, seated in the second row on the left; Benazir, seated in the second row in the center; and Naheed Khan, senior party member and Bhutto's political secretary, positioned in the second row on the right. In the back of the vehicle seated on two benches facing each other were Senator Safdar Abbasi, a senior party member, on the right bench; bodyguard Khalid Shahenshah, on the left bench; and Razaq Mirani, personal attendant of the former prime minister, on the right bench to the left of Senator Abbasi. Kaira's two vehicles on either side of Bhutto's Land Cruiser carried his men.

Chaudhry Aslam's PPP unarmed security team rode in the Vigo pick-up trucks. The black Mercedes-Benz carried the driver, PPP official Faratullah Babar, seated in the front passenger seat, and, in the rear passenger seat from left to right, PPP officials Babar Awan, Rehman Malik, and General (ret.) Tauqir Zia.

Benazir's caravan reached Faizabad Junction at about 2:15 p.m., where the Rawalpindi District Police were to assume responsibility for the convoy's security. The police security plan called for an escort composed of a traffic police "pilot" jeep, a regular police jeep leading the convoy, and three Elite Force Toyota pickup trucks protecting Bhutto's Land Cruiser on three sides. According to the passengers in her vehicle, however, there was only one traffic police vehicle.

At about 2:56 p.m., Bhutto's convoy turned right at the Murree Road–Liaquat Road junction and headed to the inner security gate into the VIP parking area at Liaquat Bagh. No one in the security team attempted to stop Bhutto from standing through the roof escape hatch of her Land Cruiser and waving at the large crowd around the vehicle while it moved slowly on Liaquat Road.

Video footage and pictures show that while Bhutto's car drove down much of Liaquat Road, it was flanked only by her private security vehicles. No Elite Force vehicle was accompanying Bhutto's Land Cruiser. Inspector Azmat Dogar, the Elite Force's commander, was in the crowd some distance from Bhutto's vehicle. The assertion by the police that they had provided a defensive box formation around her as she arrived at the rally is false, and the Elite Force unit did not execute their duties as specified in the security deployment. In short, the full escort as described by the police was not present.

Around 3:16 p.m., Bhutto's caravan had to stop for about five to six minutes at the inner gate of the parking area to wait for that gate to be opened, during which time she remained standing through the escape hatch, totally unprotected. According to the PPP, the delay in opening the gate was because the police did not have the key to it. The police, however, said that they did not want to allow the large crowd following Bhutto to get into the VIP parking area. Altogether, Bhutto stood through the escape hatch for the approximately twenty minutes it took to drive from the Murree Road–Liaquat Road junction to the gate of the parking area. Hence, Rawalpindi District Police's claim that they were surprised when Bhutto emerged from the escape hatch on her way out of Liaquat Bagh seems to be untrue.

Once the convoy went past the inner gate, around 3:23 p.m., it parked in the VIP parking area to the rear of the stage. Inside the VIP parking area were at least three vehicles: Benazir Bhutto's white Land Cruiser, Kaira's lead vehicle, and the black bulletproof Mercedes-Benz car. Temporary wooden stairs had been built to access the stage from the rear, directly from the parking area. After exiting her vehicle, Bhutto climbed the stairs to the stage, waved to the crowd, and took her seat.

Many national party leaders, security guards, and aides were on the stage surrounding Bhutto in what appeared to be an improvised setup. Also joining her on the stage were all of the parliamentary candidates from Rawalpindi District. Benazir's voice was hoarse from days of campaign rallies, and she had a slight cold. As usual, she covered her black hair with a white *dupatta.* Upon her arrival, a few party leaders warmed up the crowd, so it was already late afternoon when Bhutto finally spoke.

While Benazir listened to the opening speeches, Sherry Rehman,[3] a top media adviser and PPP leader, leaned over to whisper in Bhutto's ear that several Nawaz Sharif election workers had been killed in a gunfight at a rally elsewhere in Rawalpindi. Benazir asked to be reminded to call Nawaz to offer her condolences. Meanwhile, at the rear of the stage, as the police tried to prevent people from climbing to the crowded stage, a scuffle broke out between policemen and some young PPP activists. This created an air of tension between PPP workers and the police officers posted in that area. The police stated that the dispute was minor and was settled immediately, whereas some local PPP representatives claimed it was serious. Apparently, the policemen felt insulted and from then on they became more passive in their security duty.

Thousands of people attended the public gathering. The crowd was enthusiastic, and PPP leaders and activists considered the event to have been a great success. Benazir gave a rousing speech, one of the best of her campaign, according to observers, and they described her as having been radiant that day. She issued an impassioned call to end military rule and to defeat extremists. "The country is in danger," she said, vowing to save it with the power of the people.

The rally concluded at about 5:10 p.m., after which Bhutto descended the wooden stairs and entered her Land Cruiser. The occupants of the Land Cruiser and their positions in the vehicle were the same as during the trip into the park. In the black Mercedes-Benz car, the passengers were also the same.

STRANGELY FOR A back-up vehicle, the black bulletproof Mercedes-Benz was the first to leave the parking area. It never became clear how much distance there was between this vehicle and the rest of Bhutto's convoy at the moment of the blast. Plausible reports range from 100 to 250 meters. Some in the car told our commission that they were close enough to the former prime minister's vehicle to feel the impact of the blast. Witnesses at the site of the blast stated that the Mercedes-Benz left Liaquat Bagh so quickly that it was nowhere to be seen when the blast occurred. In fact, the commission did not see this vehicle in the many video images of the exit area it reviewed. What is more surprising is that even though some occupants of the car acknowledged that they felt the impact of the blast, and although this was the alternative vehicle in case of any emergency, the Mercedes traveled all the way to the Zardari House, a drive of twenty to thirty minutes, before the occupants became aware that Bhutto had been injured in the blast. They didn't even stop at a safe distance following the explosion to check on her condition, the condition of her vehicle, and whether the backup vehicle was needed.

Kaira's security car was the next to leave the inner parking area after the Mercedes-Benz car, with Benazir's vehicle right behind it, followed by another of Kaira's vehicles. The two Vigo pickup trucks then joined the convoy from the outer parking area located between the inner and outer gates.

At 5:12 p.m., Bhutto's Land Cruiser exited from the outer gate. Crowds of people who were already on Liaquat Road drew closer to the vehicle as it began to turn right onto the thoroughfare. The police claimed that they had not allowed anyone to leave the park before the departure of Bhutto's caravan, but video and other evidence suggest that people swirled out of the gates, swelling the crowd around the Land Cruiser. Just as it had happened during her arrival at the park, Benazir emerged through the escape hatch of the vehicle and started waving to her supporters. When the vehicle approached the central road divider, it slowed further while nosing its way through a crowd carrying banners and electoral campaign signs.

Bhutto's security people were worried that the crowd was slowing down the convoy. Major Imtiaz, sitting in the front seat of the Land Rover, wanted to call City Police Officer (CPO) Saud Aziz, Rawalpindi's police chief, by cell phone, but he did not have the police chief's direct number. Instead, he called Saud Aziz's operator and the operator at the police station in Multan, another town in Punjab Province, where Major Imtiaz had recently served. Such improvisation by Major Imtiaz evidenced a lack of professionalism.

There were discrepancies about the nature of the crowd that surrounded the Land Cruiser. Passengers in the Land Cruiser and some local PPP members recalled that they were mostly party activists, and they did not see any strange movements among them. The Rawalpindi District Police and other PPP members, however, believed that a group of people had deliberately stood in front of the Land Cruiser to prevent it from moving. Regardless of the accuracy of either account, the fact remains that the police did not manage the crowd outside of Liaquat Bagh. Thus, the attacker was able to get much closer to Bhutto's vehicle than might ordinarily have been possible.

The Rawalpindi police and some PPP workers dispute the exact exit route agreed for Bhutto's convoy. The Rawalpindi

District Police and District Coordinating Officer (DCO) Muhammad Irfan Elahi, the highest-ranking civilian bureaucrat in Rawalpindi, asserted that the planned route for the convoy was the right turn onto Liaquat Road and the left onto Murree Road, retracing the convoy's entry route. Only in case of an emergency was the convoy to make a left turn after exiting the outer gate (a decision to take the emergency route had to be made by the senior police officer in charge of security on the scene). But local PPP workers who were at the preparatory meeting with the police disagree. They claim that the original plan was to make a left turn onto Liaquat Road and that the meeting minutes provided by DCO Elahi were inaccurate. In any case, photographs show two stationary police vehicles on Liaquat Road blocking the left lane from where the left turn would have been made. Consequently, in an emergency it would have been impossible for Bhutto's convoy to use the escape route, unless those police vehicles had been quickly moved. We learned that these vehicles were official vehicles of senior Rawalpindi police officers. At the very least, it was irresponsible for these vehicles to have been parked in such a way as to block the emergency exit route.

The Rawalpindi police stated that vehicles from the Elite Force unit were waiting right outside the outer gate to escort Benazir Bhutto's convoy and that they were about to go into a protective box formation when the attack happened. However, forming the box at that point would have been impracticable, given the narrow width of Liaquat Road and the numerous people who had already started to surround Benazir's vehicle. Moreover, video footage shows scarce uniformed police on the scene available to push back the crowd to create space for the box formation. Musharraf claimed there were four police vehicles with thirty police officers flanking Bhutto's vehicle, plus one thousand policemen deployed at the rally.[4] But video and photographs taken shortly before the blast, as well as commission interviews, indicate that the Elite Force unit was not in place either at the entry or at the exit of the convoy, thus failing manifestly in its duty to afford protection.

Having exited the outer gate, the Land Cruiser started to make a right turn onto Liaquat Road. As it crept toward the central divider on Liaquat Road, the crowd began chanting political slogans. It's not clear if Bhutto made the decision to stand up on her own or was urged to do so. Before she stood up, Benazir asked Naheed Khan to make a phone call to Nawaz Sharif, PML-N leader, to convey condolences for the deaths of some of his supporters who had been shot during a PML-N rally earlier that day, also in Rawalpindi. The press had informed that the shooting incident occurred between supporters of the PML-N and those of the PML-Q.

While Khan was trying to reach Sharif, Benazir, seeing the enthusiastic crowd, stopped her and asked Senator Abbasi, who was sitting in one of the rear seats, to chant slogans to respond to the multitude using the vehicle's loudspeaker. Bhutto then stood on the seat and appeared through the escape hatch, her head and shoulders exposed.[5]

Benazir waved to the people. The vehicle continued to move slowly into its right turn onto Liaquat Road. At this point, a man wearing dark glasses appeared in the crowd on the left side of the Land Cruiser. Around 5:14 p.m., while the vehicle continued into its slow right turn, the man pulled out a pistol and, from a distance of approximately two to three meters, fired three shots at Bhutto. Scotland Yard determined, by analyzing video, that the three shots were fired in less than one second.

Video footage taken from a back angle shows Bhutto's *dupatta* and hair flick upward after the second shot. However, there is no evidence of a link between the second shot and that movement. After the third shot, she started to descend into the vehicle. The gunman lowered the gun, looked down, and then detonated the explosives attached to his body.

When the gunman activated his suicide vest, he was near the left rear corner of the vehicle, and video footage shows that the Land Cruiser was still making the right turn. The Scotland Yard team's analysis shows that it took 1.6 seconds from the time of the first shot to the detonation of the bomb.

Naheed Khan, who had been sitting to Benazir's right, recalled that immediately after she heard the three gunshots, Bhutto fell down into the vehicle, the right side of her head coming to rest on Khan's lap. The right side of Bhutto's head was bleeding profusely, and blood was trickling out of her ear. She was not moving. Makhdoom Amin Fahim, who sat to Benazir's left, remembered that Bhutto fell heavily and showed no sign of life after that. According to Scotland Yard's analysis, the flash of the blast appeared just over two-thirds of a second after Bhutto disappeared from view. No one else in her vehicle was seriously injured.

In the wake of the blast, the scene was one of shock, fear, and confusion; there was little, if any, police control. The site was filled with blood and smoke. The bomb, wrapped with ball bearings, had killed or injured dozens of people. The crime scene was not immediately cleared and cordoned off.

Senator Abbasi told the driver to head to the hospital, initially having in mind a hospital in Islamabad. The district hospital had Benazir Bhutto's blood type ready in case of an emergency and was quite near the crime scene. However, the driver headed to the Rawalpindi General Hospital (RGH), as no one instructed him otherwise. Although all four of its tires were punctured by the blast, the Land Cruiser managed to drive along Liaquat Road for approximately three hundred meters toward the junction with Murree Road where it turned left. The Land Cruiser moved along Murree Road on the metal rims of the wheels, but the driver managed to keep the vehicle moving for several kilometers. The Land Cruiser made a U-turn at the Rehmanabad junction, located approximately four kilometers from the Liaquat Road–Murree Road junction, in order to get to the other side of the road where RGH was located.

At this point, there was only one traffic police vehicle ahead of the Land Cruiser. No other vehicles were visible—neither the bulletproof black Mercedes-Benz nor any Elite Force unit vehicles. There was no ambulance available either. The head of the Elite commando unit declared that two Elite vehicles attempted to follow Bhutto's Land Cruiser, but that they couldn't move because of the injured and dead people in front of the two vehicles. Following the U-turn, the Land Cruiser stalled. The group had to wait for some time on Murree Road until a private vehicle that was following, belonging to PPP leader Sherry Rehman, arrived and transported Bhutto to the hospital. It took about thirty-four minutes for Benazir and her companions to reach RGH.

Soon after the blast outside Liaquat Bagh, chief police officer Saud Aziz left the crime scene for the hospital. Policeman Yaseen Farooq followed soon thereafter, while the most senior police official remaining at the crime scene was the deputy police chief Khurram Shahzad.

The alternate bulletproof black Mercedes drove to the Zardari House, where it arrived about half an hour after the attack. Security adviser Rehman Malik phoned his brother-in-law, who told Malik that Benazir had ducked into her vehicle and he thought she was unharmed. But, as the backup vehicle, the Mercedes-Benz car would have been an essential element of Bhutto's convoy on the return trip, even if the occupants of that car had ascertained that she had been unscathed in the attack. The Mercedes passengers made a stop before arriving at the Zardari House to ask a policeman for further information. Over the police radio, Malik and the others in the Mercedes learned that Benazir had been injured and possibly taken to a hospital. Despite that alarming information, they continued on to the Zardari House. Perhaps the Mercedes passengers were worried that a second bomb might go off, as had happened in other terrorist attacks.

AT RAWALPINDI GENERAL Hospital (later renamed Benazir Bhutto Hospital), Bhutto was received by medical personnel from the Accident and Emergency Department. It was around 5:40 p.m. In the resuscitation room, she was treated by Dr. Saeeda Yasmin. Hospital staff were also busy treating victims of the shooting at the Nawaz Sharif rally earlier that day.

Bhutto was pale, unconscious, and not breathing. There was a wound to the right of her head from which blood was trickling and whitish matter was visible. Her clothes were soaked in blood. Dr. Saeeda immediately began efforts to resuscitate her. Dr. Aurangzeb Khan, the senior registrar, joined Dr. Saeeda to assist. Both doctors said that they did not observe any other injury. As there was no improvement in Bhutto's condition, the doctors moved her to the operating room located on the second floor to continue resuscitation efforts, aided by other medical personnel.

At around 5:50 p.m., Professor Mohammed Mussadiq Khan, the hospital's senior physician, arrived and took charge.

Mussadiq Khan is the son of the doctor who, at the same hospital, attempted—unsuccessfully—to save the life of Prime Minister Liaquat Ali Khan fifty-six years earlier, gunned down at the same park where Benazir had been attacked. The doctors still had not detected a pulse. At 5:57 p.m., Professor Mussadiq Khan opened Benazir Bhutto's chest and carried out open-heart massage, without progress.

At 6:16 p.m., Mussadiq Khan stopped resuscitation efforts and declared the former prime minister dead. He ordered all of the men to leave the room so that the female doctors and nurses could clean the body. Strictly medical personnel had been in the operating room until then.

Dr. Qudsiya Anjum Qureshi cleaned Bhutto's head, neck, and upper body and checked Bhutto's body for further injury. She saw no wounds other than the one to the right side of her head and the thoracotomy wound. Bhutto was then dressed in hospital clothing and her clothes given to her maid. The doctors stated that they had not seen her *dupatta*, which remains missing to this day.

On three different occasions, Professor Mussadiq Khan asked Police Chief Saud Aziz for permission to conduct an autopsy on Benazir Bhutto, but Aziz denied each request. At the second request, Aziz is reported to have sarcastically asked the professor whether a criminal complaint had been filed yet, a matter in the chief of police's area of competence, not that of the doctor. Rawalpindi's top civilian authority, DCO Muhammad Irfan Elahi, had arrived at the hospital and was present outside the operating room. Elahi supported Saud Aziz's denial of permission for an autopsy. All authorities present justified the refusal to allow an autopsy on the grounds that they wanted to get permission from Benazir's family.

Pakistani law dictates that in the case of an unnatural death, the police must have a postmortem examination report as part of their investigation. This requirement places the responsibility for initiating an examination on the police, not the hospital authorities. In fact, hospital officials must get a request from the police before proceeding. Only a district magistrate may waive the need for a postmortem examination. If the family of a deceased person declines to have a postmortem examination carried out, it must appeal to a judge for an order waiving the requirement.

There are sensitivities involved in conducting a postmortem examination on a woman in Pakistani tradition. However, due to the forensic importance of this type of examination, the police can take steps to overcome any religious or cultural objections.

Benazir Bhutto's body remained in the operating room until it was placed in a wooden coffin and removed from the hospital at about 10:35 p.m., after which it was transported to the nearby Chaklala Air Base. Around 1:00 a.m. on December 28, at Chaklala Air Base, the remains were entrusted to her husband, Asif Ali Zardari, who had just flown in from Dubai and signed an acknowledgment note.

Police Chief Saud Aziz denied to our commission that the doctors had repeatedly requested his permission for a postmortem examination and told us that because of Benazir Bhutto's importance, he could not just have an autopsy performed without first seeking her family's consent. He first sought the approval of the president of the PPP, Makhdoom Amin Fahim, for an examination. Fahim told him that he could not give such approval and asked him to wait for Asif Ali Zardari, who was on his way to Pakistan from Dubai. When Zardari arrived at Chaklala Air Base, the request for permission was made to him, and he declined.

The commission found it remarkable that Bhutto's remains were moved to Chaklala Air Base in Rawalpindi before Zardari's arrival from Dubai. The note signed by Zardari accepting his wife's remains is date-stamped 1:10 a.m. on December 28, but as mentioned, the body was removed from the hospital around 10:35 p.m. the night before. If the police were genuinely waiting for Zardari's permission before requesting a postmortem examination, they should have kept Bhutto's body at the hospital. Instead, they moved her remains to the air base, thereby rendering such an examination more difficult. When questioned about this, senior Punjab officials stated that the plan was to carry out the examination at the base, which also had medical facilities. However, Bhutto's coffin was not taken to the medical facilities but instead was placed in a regular room at the base.

Rawalpindi police chief Saud Aziz sent several memos to his superiors regarding the absence of a postmortem examination. The memos and a subsequent letter by Punjab authorities place the blame on Zardari's refusal to approve an autopsy, also portraying that refusal in misleading terms. The letter is clearly intended to hide Aziz's fundamental omission to carry out his legal obligation regarding the autopsy. Zardari was confronted with an impossible situation, one that almost compelled him to refuse the request for an autopsy, given that the body had been placed in a coffin and that no autopsy had been carried out although five hours had passed since Bhutto had been declared dead. There was a clear intent to shift responsibilities and perpetrate a cover-up of the true reasons behind not conducting a postmortem examination. Such preconceived efforts and justifications indicated that Aziz did not act independently on this matter.

Considering that he could not obtain police consent to carry out an autopsy, Professor Mussadiq Khan called in X-ray technician Ghafoor Jadd, who took two X-rays of Bhutto's skull with a portable X-ray machine. He did this without notifying or seeking the approval of Saud Aziz.

ISI Rawalpindi detachment commander, Colonel Jehangir Akhtar, was present at the hospital through much of the evening. At one point, the ISI deputy director general, Major General Nusrat Naeem, contacted Professor Mussadiq Khan by calling Colonel Jehangir's cell phone. When asked about this by the commission, Naeem initially denied making any calls to the hospital; but when pressed further, he acknowledged that he had indeed phoned the hospital to hear directly from Professor Mussadiq Khan that Bhutto had died. He did this before reporting to his superiors.

Bhutto's death certificate was completed and signed by the senior registrar, Dr. Aurangzeb, who recorded the cause of death as "To be determined on autopsy."

MANY PPP MEMBERS asserted publicly and in private shortly after the assassination that Bhutto had been shot. Some PPP members told us that at least one of the doctors had initially stated that Bhutto had suffered gunshot injuries, implying that the doctors must have deliberately altered their findings subsequently. The commission was unable to find any basis to support this view, however honestly held. Rather, some doctors did indeed acknowledge that they considered the existence of gunshot injuries early in their efforts to resuscitate Bhutto but ruled that out in their final assessment. There is one doctor who arrived during the evening at RGH who continues to assert that there was a gunshot wound. He was not, however, an examining doctor and did not base his views on direct observation of a gunshot injury.

The commission also interviewed some PPP supporters who had been injured in the blast. None had received bullet wounds, as previously reported in some media reports. According to the police, over twenty-five people were also interviewed in the immediate aftermath of the attack, and none received bullet wounds. They were instead injured by ball bearings.

During the course of the investigation, the commission was not provided with any credible, new information showing that Benazir Bhutto had received bullet wounds. Senior PPP official Sherry Rehman, who had earlier publicly asserted that she had seen Bhutto's gunshot injuries, retracted that statement when interviewed by the commission. In fact, she had not seen Bhutto's head wound and had been advised to tell the media that she had seen bullet wounds. Although Benazir Bhutto's followers may have justifiably assumed that the former prime minister had been shot in the confusion surrounding the attack, the continued assertion that she had been shot, without evidence, as well as the assertion of untrue eyewitness accounts, was and remains misleading.

On the afternoon of December 28, in Sindh Province, Benazir Bhutto was laid to rest in her family's mausoleum at Garhi Khuda Baksh in Larkana. Her death was followed by enormous grief and anger among her supporters. As riots spread across Pakistan, police confirmed that thirty-eight people had died in clashes, fifty-three had suffered injuries and that more than seventy vehicles had been set on fire by protesters in Karachi alone. They also reported that Bhutto supporters had raided a police station in Peshawar, resulting in gunfire injuries to several police officers; that a train had been set on fire in the town of Tando Jam; and that there had been numerous attacks on banks, state-run grocery stores and election offices belonging to Musharraf's party. Many believed that a generation's hopes of building a stable democracy in Pakistan had died with Benazir Bhutto.

Heraldo Muñoz (the author and head of the UN Commission of Inquiry) and Commissioner Peter Fitzgerald (left) meeting with Interior Minister Rehman Malik, former Benazir Bhutto security adviser and lead government point person during the investigation.

8

Whodunit?

On the evening of December 28, the day after the assassination of Benazir Bhutto, Brigadier General (ret.) Javed Iqbal Cheema, spokesperson for the Ministry of the Interior, gave a televised press conference to set out the cause of her death as well as to name those responsible for the attack. He announced that Bhutto had died from a head injury sustained when hitting her head on the lever of the specially designed escape hatch of the vehicle and that Baitullah Mehsud, in association with Al-Qaida, was responsible for the attack. As evidence, he presented an intercepted telephone conversation in Pashto between Mehsud and one Maulvi Sahib, in which Mehsud was heard congratulating Maulvi on "a spectacular job."[1]

General Musharraf had decided to authorize the press conference during a meeting on the morning of December 28 at a facility in the general headquarters known as Camp House. That meeting, at which Musharraf was briefed on the intercept and on medical evidence, was attended by the directors general of the ISI, MI, and IB. Brigadier Cheema was summoned to a subsequent meeting at the ISI headquarters, where he was instructed by the director general of the ISI to hold the press conference. The ISI provided the information the spokesperson was to relay.[2] In attendance at this second meeting, in addition to Brigadier Cheema, were Interior Secretary Kamal Shah, the director general of the ISI, the director general of the IB, the deputy director of the ISI, and another ISI brigadier general.

According to the government the evidence for the cause of death was clear: Video footage showed that the shooter's bullets did not hit Bhutto. Through Brigadier General Cheema, the government concluded that she must have hit her head on the lever of the vehicle's escape hatch—or "sun roof," as mistakenly described in news reports.

The press conference was met with widespread public outrage and media skepticism in Pakistan. The PPP and others accused the government of a cover-up.

Many expressed doubts about the sudden and timely appearance of the telephone intercept as well as the speed with which its contents were analyzed and interpreted. One senior policeman we interviewed during our investigation declared about the phone intercept, "In 24 years of service, I have never seen such spontaneous appearance of evidence." Many also challenged the version that Bhutto had not been shot and questioned how quickly that purported analysis had been done. Numerous senior PPP officials believed the government was clearly suggesting, in an effort to demean Benazir Bhutto, that she had caused her own death by emerging from her vehicle to salute the crowd.

The morning following the assassination, the doctors who treated Benazir Bhutto were convened at the hospital by DCO Muhammad Irfan Elahi, the main civilian bureaucrat in the district under the authority of Punjab Province. Elahi demanded that the doctors submit a report concerning the treatment given to Bhutto. He told the doctors to bring the original to him directly and further instructed them to retain neither hard copies nor electronic copies of the report. A request for such a report had never been made before this incident, nor has there been one since. The report was prepared and submitted to DCO Elahi. On the afternoon of December 28, Professor Mussadiq Khan gave a brief press conference following orders given by Elahi, who received his instructions from the home secretary of Punjab Province.

When a terrorist offense has been committed, Pakistan's Anti-terrorism Act requires the establishment of a joint investigation team (JIT). This type of investigation allows various agencies—whether law enforcement or intelligence—to work together. In terrorism cases, either the provincial police or the federal government can initiate a JIT. When a province initiates a JIT, the provincial government takes the lead in selecting the team members. Due to the expertise of the Special Investigation Group of the Federal Investigation Agency (FIA), the FIA generally assigns some of its officers from that section to JITs.

On December 28, the authorities of Punjab Province established a JIT, headed by Additional Inspector General (AIG) Abdul Majeed. In addition to police officials from Punjab, the investigative group included three senior members of the FIA, including an explosives expert, a senior Criminal Investigation Department police officer at the rank of deputy inspector general, an expert on forensic photography, and nine middle-ranked police officers. At the time the joint investigation team was set up, Majeed was out of the country, so for the first three days, the JIT was led by the next most senior police officer on the team.

On the evening of December 28, members of the group

went to Police Lines—an administrative center of the Rawalpindi District Police that includes barracks and other facilities—where they met police chief Saud Aziz. Instead of proceeding directly to the crime site, Saud Aziz served tea for the investigators in a conference room. While the JIT members were still in the conference room, the television aired the press conference given by Brigadier Cheema. The police chief rhetorically asked the JIT members what they intended to investigate, since the perpetrator had been already identified by the government. When the JIT members pressed him to visit the crime scene, Saud Aziz responded that since it was already dark, he would arrange for a visit to the scene the next morning.

The following day, the investigators returned to Police Lines, where they were able to examine Bhutto's vehicle. They soon discovered that there was no blood or tissue on the escape hatch lever that would be consistent with the gaping injury to Bhutto's head, suggesting strongly that she had not hit her head on the lever.

Following that inspection, rather than taking the investigators directly to the crime scene, CPO Saud Aziz hosted a luncheon that extended into the late afternoon, at the end of which he again suggested that it would be dark by the time the team arrived at the crime scene. It was only at around 5:00 p.m. that the JIT investigators were taken to the crime scene at Liaquat Bagh. In short, the investigators were not able to conduct on-site investigations until two full days after the assassination. Once at the scene, after Aziz's delaying tactics, the investigators realized that it had been hosed down.

On the evening of the twenty-seventh, Saud Aziz had left the crime scene for Rawalpindi General Hospital, but Deputy Police Chief Khurram Shahzad, the most senior Rawalpindi police official in charge at the crime scene, continued to take instructions from Aziz by telephone. Despite the fact that the crime scene was not immediately sealed, the police were able to collect some evidence. Officers from several intelligence agencies were also present and collected evidence using, as one Rawalpindi police officer told us, better evidence-collection equipment than the police. Within one hour and forty minutes of the blast, however, Khurram ordered the fire and rescue officials present to wash the crime scene down with fire hoses. He told the commission that the police had collected all the available evidence by then. Police records show that only twenty-three pieces of evidence were collected, in a case where one would normally have expected thousands. The evidence included mostly human body parts, two pistols, spent cartridges, and Bhutto's damaged vehicle.

Khurram and other senior Rawalpindi police officers justified hosing down the crime scene as a necessary "crowd control measure." They claimed that PPP supporters at the scene were highly agitated when they learned that Benazir had died and that some of them could have become disruptive. The policemen added that Bhutto supporters were smearing blood on themselves and that, therefore, the police needed to wash away the blood as a public order measure. But after being further interrogated by us, Khurram admitted that he saw only one person involved in such desperate behavior.

Even police officials familiar with the case disputed the assertion that there was a public order problem in Rawalpindi. They further disagreed that the presence of an unruly crowd would prevent the establishment of police barricades around the crime scene and justify hosing it down. In fact, at Rawalpindi General Hospital, where many grieving PPP supporters later gathered, the disturbance was minimal.

Before issuing the order to hose down the scene, Khurram

called his superior, Saud Aziz, to seek permission, which was granted. Sources, including police officials familiar with the case, have doubted Khurram's claim that the hosing was his decision. In Pakistan, power-politics considerations condition all public institutions, even more so when there is a high-profile political case, making police officers particularly sensitive to superior orders.

Police officials declared that hosing down a crime scene is extraordinarily and fundamentally inconsistent with Pakistani police practice. With the exception of some Rawalpindi policemen, nearly all senior Pakistani police officials we interviewed criticized the manner in which this crime scene was managed. One senior policeman told us that hosing down the crime scene amounted to "criminal negligence."

I am convinced that Police Chief Saud Aziz did not act independently in deciding to hose down the crime scene. One source, speaking on the basis of anonymity, told us that Aziz had received a call from the army headquarters instructing him to order the cleanup of the crime scene. Another source, also speaking on the basis of anonymity, said that Aziz was ordered to hose down the scene by Major General Nadeem Ijaz Ahmed, then director general of the MI. In this case, as on many occasions during the commission's inquiry, individuals, including government officials, expressed fear or hesitation to speak openly about who could have ordered the hosing down of the scene. The only precedents for hosing down a crime scene involved military targets. Some police officials saw this as further indication that the military was involved.

The controversy surrounding the washing down of the crime scene was so intense that the chief minister of Punjab set up a committee of inquiry, composed of three senior Punjab officials, to look into the matter. The Punjab committee possessed a limited mandate: inquire into the circumstances leading to the washing down of the scene, determine whether it was done in bad faith, and determine whether it posed any difficulty in reaching a conclusion on the cause of death.

The committee started its investigation on February 14, 2008, and concluded its work the very next day. It accepted the Rawalpindi police explanation that the decision to wash the crime scene was implemented by Khurram, the police officer at the scene, with permission from Saud Aziz on the grounds of public order. It further found that the decision was not made in bad faith and that hosing down the crime scene did not negatively affect the conclusion as to the cause of death.

The Punjab committee investigation was clearly a whitewash of the actions of the Rawalpindi police in failing to manage the crime scene and destroying evidence. Beyond the hosing down of the crime scene, there were more serious questions regarding the preservation of evidence.

Bhutto's Land Cruiser was initially taken to the city police station after midnight early on December 28 and then taken to Police Lines. In the early hours of December 28, Police Chief Aziz went to Police Lines, together with the ISI officers who had first conducted a forensic examination of the vehicle. An investigating police officer, on the orders of Saud Aziz, removed Benazir Bhutto's shoes and took them back to the city police station. Sometime later, an order went out to return the shoes to the car. Evidently, such actions interfered with the integrity of the evidence. The same policeman who was ordered to remove the shoes from the vehicle testified that he saw brain matter on a window and on the car's seat. Moreover, while the vehicle was parked at Police Lines, it was not properly preserved. The commission was told that during a visit by some JIT members, people were cleaning the Land Cruiser, even though investigations were still ongoing. When the investigative team carried out its physical examination of the vehicle, they did not find any hair, blood, or other matter on the lip of the escape hatch. Forensic analyses of swabs of the lip of the escape hatch later carried out by the JIT and Scotland Yard also found nothing. Such interference would naturally have damaged any evidence present.

Once the investigators arrived at the scene, they readily saw that it had been hosed down. Despite the late hour of their arrival, they spent seven hours there. They followed the water current, wading through the drainage sewer and collecting evidence from the debris. They were able to recover one bullet casing from the drainage sewer, later established through forensic examination to have been fired from the pistol bearing the bomber's DNA. The detectives left the scene around midnight. The Rawalpindi police provided security for them, cordoning off the road while they were there. The next day, the team returned to continue the search. Upon their request, the scene remained cordoned off and the road closed. They eventually recovered other evidence in the course of their crime scene examination, including a piece of the suicide bomber's skull from atop one of the buildings near the site.

On December 31, Inspector General Majeed resumed the command of the JIT. This change shifted the internal dynamics of the investigating team. Majeed sidelined the senior and more experienced officers who had started the investigation and dealt directly with the most junior investigators. Two senior officers invited to join the JIT from the Sindh police decided to return to their province after only two days under the new leadership. Much of the work carried out by the JIT from this point on was shaped by information Majeed received from the intelligence agencies, which retained sole control over the sharing of information with the police, providing it on a selective basis.

It is my belief that the police deliberately botched the investigation into Bhutto's assassination. Some police officials did not execute their professional duties as vigorously as they should have, perhaps fearing the involvement in the crime of powerful actors or intelligence agents. At a minimum, the Rawalpindi police, as well as the Punjab administration and the federal government, failed to take the necessary measures to protect the former prime minister, though knowing that she faced fresh and urgent security risks.

ON A CLOUDY London day at the beginning of September 2009, my fellow commissioners and I walked into the Scotland Yard headquarters building for a full day of meetings. We were there to work with the detectives who had participated in a forensic inquiry shortly after Benazir Bhutto's assassination. The Musharraf government had been forced by an outraged public to agree to an outside investigation to ascertain the cause of death. Musharraf and UK prime minister Gordon Brown decided that a team of forensic experts and detectives from the Metropolitan Police Counter Terrorism Command (SO15) would carry out a limited inquiry to assist the Pakistani police investigation into Bhutto's assassination.

The team of Scotland Yard experts and investigators arrived in Pakistan on January 4, 2008, and spent two and a half weeks carrying out their investigation. The team concluded that although it was not possible to "categorically . . . exclude the possibility of there being a gunshot wound . . . the available evidence suggested there was no gunshot injury."[3] The London metropolitan police team also found that Benazir Bhutto had died of a severe head injury caused by impact on the escape hatch lip as a direct result of the blast and that the same individual both fired the shots and detonated the explosives. Given the narrow focus of the Scotland Yard inquiry, such a conclusion was unsurprising. Dr. Nathaniel Cary, the pathologist appointed by Scotland Yard, confirmed that the force of the blast caused Bhutto's fatal injury and that said injury was indeed a result of striking her head on the lip of the escape hatch opening rather than on the latch, as announced by the Ministry of the Interior in the press conference on December 28, 2007.

Our commission asked the Netherlands Forensic Institute (NFI) to conduct a review of Scotland Yard's investigation of the cause and manner of Bhutto's death. The NFI analyzed the Scotland Yard report and concluded that there were no significant inconsistencies in its investigation.

The scientific analysis of the suicide bomber's remains—graphic pictures of which we saw at Scotland Yard—established that he was a teenage male, younger than sixteen years of age. According to the Pakistani investigations, this young man was named Bilal—and also known as Saeed—and was from South Waziristan. But beyond the actual identity of the suicide bomber, great mystery remained about his background and whom he was working for.

According to the Musharraf government, Bilal had acted on the orders of Baitullah Mehsud, a Taliban commander from South Waziristan[4] and veteran of the anti-Soviet jihad of the 1980s. This assertion, that Baitullah Mehsud was behind the assassination of Benazir Bhutto, was premature at best. Such a hasty announcement prejudiced the police investigations, which had not yet begun at the time of the press conference in which Mehsud was named the mastermind of the attack.

The communication intercepted by the ISI implicating

Mehsud is purported to have been a telephone conversation between Emir Sahib (said to be Baitullah Mehsud) and Maulvi Sahib. In it, the two speakers congratulate each other on an event that government spokesman Brigadier Cheema asserted was the assassination. Members of the ISI stated that they already had the voice signature of Baitullah Mehsud and were in a position to identify his voice on the intercept. The conversation did not mention Bhutto by name. The commission did not have access to the actual recording—only a transcript of it—and could not evaluate the authenticity of the purported intercept.

It is not clear how or when the intercept from the ISI was recorded. A former senior ISI official told our commission that the ISI had been tracking Baitullah Mehsud's communications closely and was, therefore, poised to intercept the call. He also asserted that the ISI had been tracking Taliban-linked terrorist cells that were closely pursuing Bhutto, targeting her at a series of successive public gatherings. According to this ISI official, it was one of these cells that executed the assassination of Benazir Bhutto in Rawalpindi.

The original JIT constituted on December 28 under the Anti-terrorism Act to look into the assassination arrested five individuals: Aitzaz Shah, Sher Zaman, Husnain Gul, Muhammad Rafaqat, and Rasheed Ahmed. In addition, the JIT charged Nasrullah Abdullah, Baitullah Mehsud, and Maulvi Sahib as "proclaimed offenders."[5]

The accused were alleged to have served as handlers and logistics supporters of the suicide bomber, or as persons who were knowledgeable about the plans to assassinate Bhutto but had failed to report such plans to the police. The charges against them included aiding and abetting terrorism, murder, and concealing information about the commission of a crime.

Investigations focused on the alleged role of these low-level individuals. Little to no focus was placed on investigating those further up the hierarchy in the planning and execution of the assassination. Surprisingly, the JIT did nothing to build a case against Mehsud, treating the contents of the intercept presented publicly by Brigadier Cheema as determinative of his culpability.

The media reported that Baitullah Mehsud denied responsibility for the assassination. Senator Saleh Shah Qureshi from South Waziristan told our commission that Mehsud had categorically denied any involvement in the Karachi assassination attempt of October 18 and the subsequent assassination of Bhutto on December 27, throwing into question the authenticity of the telephone intercept. The JIT took no steps to investigate the veracity of any such denial. Rather, some Musharraf government officials simply asserted that such denials coming from a terrorist could have no credibility. Interestingly, specialized observers told our commission that at the time, the Pakistani Taliban had not demonstrated the capacity to perpetrate an operation outside the tribal areas, such as the one that cost the life of Benazir Bhutto.

Baitullah Mehsud and the Pakistani Taliban were, undoubtedly, a clear threat to Benazir Bhutto. Just before her return to Pakistan in October 2007, a news article stated that Mehsud had threatened to welcome Bhutto with a wave of suicide bombers.[6] The report identified Senator Saleh Shah as the source, but he denied the news version emphatically. On December 29, 2007, Mehsud, through a spokesman in South Waziristan, denied his involvement in Benazir's assassination: "Neither Baitullah Mehsud nor any of his associates were involved . . . because raising your hand against women is against our tribal values and customs. Only those people who stood to gain politically are involved . . . It is a conspiracy by government, military and intelligence agencies,"[7] said Mehsud's spokesman.

However, Baitullah Mehsud had more than a reasonable motive for killing Bhutto. He was convinced that Benazir's impending return to Pakistan was part of a power-sharing deal with General Musharraf that would strengthen the already-solid pro-Americanism of the Pakistani government and thus undermine the Pakistani Taliban's power in South Waziristan. Mehsud was also certain that her secularism and moderation would hinder the Pakistani Taliban's ability to spread Islamic radicalism, aside from the fact she was a woman and considered a Shia.

The Pakistani Taliban is an agglomeration of Pashtun militant Islamist groups operating in the tribal areas. They are closely aligned with the Afghan Taliban and with Al-Qaida. Several of these groups banded together in late 2007 to form the Tehrik-e-Taliban Pakistan (TTP) under Baitullah Mehsud's leadership. Baitullah's growing power was so significant that the Musharraf government signed a peace deal with him in February 2005, which he declared null in August 2007. In March 2009 the US government offered a $5 million reward for information on Mehsud, described as a key Al-Qaida facilitator.[8]

Al-Qaida claimed responsibility for the murder of Benazir Bhutto through a statement by commander Abu al-Yazid, who stated that Al-Qaida's second-in-command, Ayman al-Zawahiri, had ordered the killing. "We terminated the most precious American asset which vowed to defeat [the] mujahedeen,"[9] declared al-Yazid, a claim he repeated by phone to the online publication *Asia Times*.[10]

During a conversation on February 24, 2010, then prime minister Gilani told my colleague commissioners and me about a meeting he had with President George W. Bush at the White House in mid-2008, where the subject of Bhutto's murder was addressed.

"As soon as I entered the Oval Office," said Gilani, "Bush

shot, 'How come you are letting Baitullah Mehsud be interviewed on Pakistani TV? Don't you know that he's the one who killed Benazir Bhutto?'"

"Then why haven't you taken him out with your drones?" Gilani responded.

Indeed, the US government seemed to believe that Mehsud was responsible. Then director of the US CIA Michael Hayden advanced in a *Washington Post* interview on January 18, 2008, that Bhutto had been killed by fighters allied with Baitullah Mehsud, with support from Al-Qaida's terrorist network.[11] The US government did not permit our commission to meet with US intelligence officials to ascertain the basis for Hayden's assertion. In any case, Bush and the US military had their eye on Mehsud. In September 2009, a US Predator drone strike killed Mehsud and his wife in South Waziristan.

BENAZIR BHUTTO KNEW there were potential assassins waiting for her, but she did not suspect just one single figure or group. Baitullah Mehsud's Pakistani Taliban was not the sole radical group that had a motive to kill her. She had received information before her return to Pakistan on October 18, 2007, that there were three other suicide bomber squads in addition to Mehsud's that would attempt to kill her: a squad linked to Hamza bin Laden, a son of Osama bin Laden; one made up of Red Mosque militants; and another from a Karachi-based militant group. But she was convinced that these terrorists would not act alone. She feared the militants could be activated by their handlers, high up in the structures of Pakistani power—specifically by militant sympathizers within the Musharraf government.

The various jihadi organizations in Pakistan are Sunni groups based largely in Punjab. Members of these groups aided the Taliban effort in Afghanistan at the behest of the ISI and later cultivated ties with Al-Qaida and Pakistani Taliban groups. A common characteristic of these jihadi groups is their adherence to the Deobandi Sunni sect of Islam and their strong anti-Shia bias.

The Lashkar-e-Taiba (LeT), or Army of the Righteous, has become, in the opinion of experts, more dangerous than Al-Qaida.[12] Despite the fact that the LeT, its charitable front organization Jamaat-ud-Dawa, and its main leaders have been included on a sanctions list by the UN Security Council, the group operates relatively freely in Pakistan.

Also operating in Pakistan is the crime family known as the "Haqqani network," Afghan members of the Zadran tribe based in the town of Miranshah in Pakistan's tribal area, where they have set up a mini empire with front companies throughout Pakistan. Raising money from wealthy donors in Gulf States, in addition to extortion, smuggling, and kidnappings, the network of about fifteen thousand fighters is led by former mujahideen commander Jalaluddin Haqqani and his two sons Badruddin and Sirajuddin, both considered more committed Islamists than their father.[13]

The Haqqanis are close to the ISI, which considers them strategic allies in any eventual war with India, Pakistan's long-term and principal foe. The ISI has recognized ties to the Haqqanis but specifies that the network has three components and that the ISI does not maintain contacts with the "militant wing."[14] The Haqqanis enjoy freedom of movement in Pakistan and have been spotted in plain sight at different public events. But beyond the fact that they are an asset of the intelligence agencies, the Haqqanis have their own agenda, have close ties to Al-Qaida, and support the Pakistani Taliban in their confrontation with the Pakistani military.

In September 2012, after much reflection, Washington designated the Haqqani network as a terrorist organization to impose sanctions on the group and its material supporters. Meanwhile, several individuals in the network had already been designated as terrorists, and more than fifty members of the Haqqani extended family, including one of Jalaluddin's sons, had been killed by American drone strikes. Ironically, in the '80s, the Haqqanis were US allies in the anti-Soviet war in Afghanistan. The famous US congressman Charlie Wilson, who made the mujahideen his cause, even called the elder Haqqani "goodness personified."[15]

Given this background, it is not surprising that such radical groups posed a real threat to Benazir Bhutto. Bhutto was not only a modern politician and the leader of a major secular party; she also rejected the extremist version of Islam espoused by these groups. In addition, she was supportive of the priority placed by Washington on the fight against terrorism, and it was public knowledge that the United Kingdom and the United States were aiding her return to Pakistan. And notwithstanding her differences with General Musharraf, she had supported his crackdown on militants, despite repeatedly castigating Musharraf for doing a halfhearted job on the terror front and for seeking deals with the Taliban. "General Musharraf's team has relied on the principle that to catch a thief you send a thief," she told a veteran journalist.[16] Bhutto's gender was also an issue for the religious extremists, who believed that a woman should not lead an Islamic country. Lastly, some militants perceived her as a Shia because her mother and husband are Shia. But threats to Bhutto came from sources well beyond Baitullah Mehsud and the militant groups that wanted to see her dead. Benazir deeply distrusted, and even feared, the so-called Establishment.

"THE ESTABLISHMENT" IS the term used in Pakistan to refer to those who exercise de facto power: the powers that be. It includes the military high command and the intelligence agencies, together with the top leadership of certain political parties, high-level members of the bureaucracy, and business individuals who are allied with them. The military high command and intelligence agencies are the core and most influential components of the Establishment.

Through her writing and public statements, Bhutto had denounced key elements of the Establishment, whose tactics and reach she knew well. She, and many others, held the military and the intelligence agencies responsible for a number of "dirty" campaigns against her when she ran for office in the 1980s and 1990s, as well as for orchestrating the sacking of her governments. She believed that the policies she stood for—a return to civilian rule and democracy, human rights, greater oversight on the nuclear program, negotiations with India, reconciliation with the non-Muslim world, and confrontation with radical Islamists—threatened the Establishment's control over Pakistan.

Benazir's and her party's manifesto for 2007 called for restrictions on the power of the military and intelligence agencies. She proposed bringing them under civilian, democratic oversight, with provisions for transparency and control of the military budget and spending. She vowed publicly to use reforms to rid the intelligence agencies of elements driven by political or religious motives.

Establishment actors threatened by her return to an active political life in Pakistan included, in particular, those who maintain sympathetic links with radical Islamists, especially the militant jihadi and Taliban groups. The ISI cultivated these relationships, initially within the context of the Cold War and the anti-Soviet war in Afghanistan in the 1980s and later in support of Kashmiri insurgents. After the Karachi bomb attack in October 2007, Benazir suggested a "larger conspiracy" involving "elements from within the Pakistani intelligence service" [17] that had created and nurtured the Taliban and the high-level individuals displeased with her return. Two Establishment figures that particularly concerned her were Lieutenant General (ret.) Hamid Gul and Brigadier (ret.) Ijaz Shah. She went so far as to name Gul and Shah outright in her October 16 letter to General Musharraf.

Gul was director general of the MI under Zia ul-Haq and then director general of the ISI when Benazir was prime minister in 1988–1990. Although he was retired, Bhutto believed he still maintained active ties with the jihadists. Gul, portrayed by an analyst as a "loudly religious man . . . who used to drink in moderation,"[18] refused to be interviewed by our commission. When asked by an Australian reporter about the allegations regarding his involvement in a conspiracy against Bhutto, Gul deflected blame—a typical ploy by intelligence agents—pointing to the United States: "One thing I do know is that [Bhutto] broke the pledge she made to the Americans. I've heard that as part of the American annoyance with her Cheney withdrew an agreement to provide her with 25 Blackwater people to protect her,"[19] Gul declared.

Brigadier Ijaz Shah, director general of the IB in 2007 and a former ISI officer, was a member of General Musharraf's inner circle. When Omar Saeed Sheikh, the principal individual accused in the Daniel Pearl murder case, was cornered in 2002, he requested to surrender to Brigadier Shah. Some believe this was because of Brigadier Shah's reported intelligence connections with Sheikh. Brigadier Shah vigorously denied this and told the commission that the surrender was facilitated through family ties in their home community. In

2007 conservative US columnist Robert Novak called Shah the man who had "orchestrated for two years the efforts to keep Bhutto out [of Pakistan]."[20]

Militants of particular concern to Bhutto included Qari Saifullah Akhtar, one of the founders of the extremist Harakat-ul Jihad Islami (HUJI), whom she accused of involvement in a failed coup attempt against her in 1995, during her second term. Akhtar, who was living in Pakistan when Bhutto returned from exile, was reportedly one of the ISI's main contacts with the Taliban regime in Afghanistan and is believed to have cultivated ties with Osama bin Laden. Benazir believed that Akhtar was connected to the Karachi attack against her in October 2007.

Akhtar had joined hands with Major General Zaheer ul-Islam Abbasi, a former intelligence officer, not only in an attempted coup against Benazir Bhutto in 1995 but also in an attempt to remove the army leadership. After Akhtar spent five months in jail, he was released from detention. Years later, arrested in the United Arab Emirates for plotting to murder Musharraf, he was handed over to Pakistan; but after being held in jail for a couple of years, he was quietly released by the government after the Supreme Court inquired as to his whereabouts. Arrested again in 2008 after Benazir Bhutto's murder and the posthumous publication of her book *Reconciliation*, in which she identified him as one of the individuals she feared, Akhtar was held only briefly and then let go without charge. Interestingly, the official JIT report on the Karachi terrorist attack against Benazir mentions Akhtar's trajectory, but details of his activities stop in August 2007, before the attacks in Karachi and in Rawalpindi, only resuming in January 2008, after Bhutto's assassination—someone had actually doctored the report. It was a poorly executed forgery, as the edited page is in one font and the rest in another. In August 2010, injured in a drone attack, Akhtar was arrested, given treatment in Peshawar, moved to Lahore, and freed. Punjab home minister Rana Sanaullah, the authority who freed Akhtar, declared that Qari Saifullah Akhtar could not be considered a terrorist.[21]

But it wasn't the militants that concerned Bhutto so much as their networks of connections with some authorities and the intelligence agencies. She and many others believed that the authorities could activate these connections to harm her. Benazir had noted that although Baitullah Mehsud had threatened to send suicide bombers against her, the real danger to her came from extremists within Pakistan's military establishment. "I'm worried about the threat within the government," she had declared in an October 2007 interview with *The Guardian*. "People like Baitullah Mehsud are just pawns."[22]

A MAJOR SOURCE of suspicion was the Pakistani intelligence agency. The ISI is no ordinary intelligence service. Beyond the usual duties of gathering information and conducting operations for national security objectives, the ISI throughout the history of Pakistan has formed political parties, made payments for political campaigns, rigged elections, and regularly interfered in national politics, contributing to the dismissal of democratic governments. Oftentimes, the ISI has been criticized for undertaking tasks that the police should be performing.

Experts affirm that most ISI military officers would rather conduct intelligence gathering and national security projects than get involved in politics. Many professional military officers also prefer to command troops rather than serve in the ISI. Despite the distance that some military officers keep from the ISI, the agency follows the army line of high command and is headed by a senior general; additionally, a majority of its officers are seconded regulars. The army, in turn, is a key institution of the Pakistani state driven by an ideology of nationalism, an ethos of service, honesty, and discipline.[23] Part of the problem is that repeatedly, Pakistani governments, whether democratic or not, have tended to manipulate and politicize the intelligence agencies.[24] But the bottom line is that Pakistan has suffered from an imbalance between military and civilian power.

The ISI commands respect and fear among Pakistanis and foreigners familiar with Pakistan. The ISI has a "cell" devoted to domestic affairs that maintains a database and gathers intelligence on individuals that could be considered dangerous to national security. According to an ISI source, Benazir's movements were closely monitored by the ISI and her "residences and offices were bugged."[25] Lieutenant General (ret.) Asad Durrani, in an article entitled "ISI: An Exceptional Secret Service," concurred with the view that the ISI is considered by some experts to be the "best of its kind."[26] But even Durrani, a former ISI director general, conceded that one of the ISI's principal "ailments" is "its being predominantly a military organization," given "the Army's exceptional role in Pakistani politics."[27]

When the Bhutto commission requested to interview the head of the ISI, Lieutenant General Ahmed Shuja Pasha, and army chief General Ashfaq Parvez Kayani, we were given a robust "No." In fact, although our request had been made confidentially, Rehman Malik, minister of the interior, responded publicly that we would "not be allowed access to the military officials or [intelligence] agency."[28] Pakistani media reported that Minister Malik had affirmed that the Pakistani army had "nothing to do with the Benazir assassination case."[29]

Well advised by a friendly Pakistani official, I wrote directly to General Kayani. After a number of informal conversations in which I conveyed the warning that the commissioners would not return to Pakistan if we were not given access to the ISI director general and the army chief, we were granted the interviews requested.

On the morning of February 24, 2010, we were conducted under heavy security to the well-guarded building of the ISI in Islamabad. We waited for quite some time before being given the green light to pass each security checkpoint leading to the entrance of the building, a grand hall that reminded visitors of the power housed inside.

General Pasha, the head of the ISI at the time, is a short, stocky, pleasant, and sophisticated man who received us with cordiality because—as he affirmed—he was following orders from the army chief. Pasha expressed that the ISI is "better than any rival." He clarified that the ISI "is not an investigating agency" and that any investigative work it does aims at collecting or corroborating information. In the case of Benazir's assassination, Pasha admitted, the ISI did provide information to the JIT. "Our boys are very good at certain things," General Pasha observed with undisguised pride. He added that the ISI had passed information regarding threats directly to Benazir and the Ministry of the Interior.

A former intelligence official told the commission that the ISI had conducted its own investigation of the Karachi attack and had successfully identified and detained four men who had provided logistical support. None of the police or other civilian officials interviewed by the commission regarding Karachi reported any knowledge of such detentions. The same source told us that ISI agents covering Bhutto's meeting in Liaquat Bagh on December 27 were the first ones to secure her vehicle and take photos of it after the blast, among other actions.

Members of the JIT who investigated Bhutto's assassination admitted that virtually all of their most important information, including that which led to the identification and arrest of those suspects now in prison, came from intelligence agencies. Moreover, resources to build investigative capacity, especially in terrorism cases, have gone to the intelligence agencies, while police resources and capacity lag. Indeed, in the aftermath of the attempts on General Musharraf's life, the capacity of the ISI was strengthened to allow it to engage more effectively in such investigations.

The head of the ISI reiterated a view we had heard often: Benazir had returned to Pakistan against everyone's advice. She was a target, General Pasha stated, because the Taliban "believed she had been brought back by the Americans." However, the ISI had no evidence that Baitullah Mehsud had committed the assassination. With regard to our questions about the role of the ISI in politics, Pasha was less than candid when he asserted that the "misconception" about the ISI's influence in politics was due to the fact that "in the past, political leaders made extensive use of [the] ISI for political tasks." We all smiled as he affirmed: "The ISI is no longer involved in political activities. This has changed now."

The meeting with army chief Ashfaq Parvez Kayani was unusual. He agreed to meet with me alone as chairman of the Bhutto inquiry commission, at the Army House in Rawalpindi, at night on Thursday, February 25, with no convoy of security vehicles accompanying me. I had to ride in a non-bulletproof van and was allowed only one armed UN policeman as an escort. I never knew who set those conditions, but I accepted them, over the strong protest of our security team.

General Kayani is a serious-looking military man, relatively tall, clean-shaven, with natural dark circles under his eyes. Born in Rawalpindi in 1952, he is known as a professional soldier of an independent mind; he had been elevated to the top military post after serving as director general of the ISI from 2004 to 2007, an unprecedented move for an army chief. Kayani had been named director general of the ISI after leading a successful investigation on the perpetrators of an assassination attempt against Musharraf, who became impressed with the young general then in charge of the X Corps. From then on, the ISI strengthened its criminal investigative capacity. Interestingly, Kayani had served as Benazir Bhutto's deputy military secretary in the 1980s, a fact that might partly explain his presence during the secret talks between Musharraf and Bhutto in the Emirates.

Following the tradition of his predecessors, Kayani has been involved in key political episodes from an institutional standpoint. In 2009 he personally interceded to persuade President Zardari to reinstate Chief Supreme Court Justice Iftikhar Muhammad Chaudhry, fired in 2007 by Musharraf, and to end federal rule in Punjab, thus yielding to opposition demands and solving a looming crisis.[30] In 2009 Kayani was the only Pakistani who made it to *Time*'s 2009 list of the world's most influential people.[31]

The general received me in a large and comfortable sitting area in a reception hall of his army residence. A discrete notetaker accompanied him. We began with small talk about the renovations made to the mansion. He was dressed in civilian clothes and chain-smoked cigarettes. The interview got off to a bad start when I asked about the negotiations preceding Benazir's return to Pakistan. "Why are you asking me this?" he said. I became annoyed and responded that the reason was simple: he had been present during the conversations between Musharraf and Bhutto while occupying the post of ISI chief. My feeling was that both he and I could be wasting our time. Kayani next expressed the view that Benazir should have returned by the end of the year according to what had been discussed with

Musharraf. He assured me there had been "a deal" that involved her becoming prime minister, Musharraf remaining as president, and all judicial charges against her being dropped.

General Kayani considered the performance of the Rawalpindi police after the assassination of Benazir Bhutto to have been "amateur." "If in 24 hours you don't completely secure the scene, then you lose the threads to solve a case," he said. I recalled that Kayani had done exactly that in the second bomb attack against Musharraf on December 25, 2003.

Although the Taliban hated Benazir, Kayani indicated that he was not sure that Baitullah Mehsud had organized the assassination. He believed the Musharraf government's press conference that had identified Mehsud as the culprit and offered the cause of her death the day following the killing had been "premature." "It should not have been done," he said. One cannot conclude culpability solely on a phone intercept, he noted, referring to Brigadier Cheema's press conference. Interestingly, General Kayani spoke fondly of Benazir Bhutto. "She had grown as a politician. She had matured politically," he reflected, between the time he had served in her government and the time when he met her again in Dubai for the secret Bhutto-Musharraf conversations.

It was raining when I left the Army House in Rawalpindi to return to our safe house in Islamabad. Upon arrival, I transmitted the contents of my conversation with Kayani to my colleague commissioners and staff. To our surprise, early the next morning *Dawn* newspaper had a headline that read, "U.N. Probe Team Chief Meets Kayani." The news report defined my conversation as "a courtesy call to discuss the progress made in the investigation," citing a government source.[32] The article also revealed that we had met earlier with the head of the ISI, General Pasha. Additionally, it stated that the security establishment had contacted the government to express its willingness to meet the commission, as it did not have "anything to hide," and to avoid any perception of "non-cooperation." Several other media outlets carried the story of our meeting with the ISI director general and the army chief.

The public exposure of these meetings fed suspicions held by some observers of Pakistan about the involvement of the ISI, or at least of some retired officers or rogue members of the agency, in the assassination of Benazir. Such conjectures were not unfounded. Sources within the United Kingdom's MI5 had told a newspaper that "factions within the Pakistan intelligence service might have been behind the assassination of the country's opposition leader Benazir Bhutto."[33]

Benazir had mentioned to Afghan president Hamid Karzai, when they met the morning of her assassination, that she was "very concerned about the ISI and the role they were playing in undermining her."[34] Shortly before her return to Pakistan in 2007, she had also told a senior reporter that the security apparatus needed to be reformed: "Unless that is done, it is going to be very difficult for us to dismantle the terrorist networks and the militant networks, and today they are a threat not only to other countries but to the unity and survival of Pakistan."[35] The former prime minister had had a major run-in with the ISI back in the late 1980s when she attempted to take control of it by removing General Hamid Gul and replacing him with retired general Shamsur Rahman Kallu. This backfired when the chief of army staff transferred the ISI's duties to the MI, then headed by Brigadier Asad Durrani, General Gul's deputy. After Benazir was dismissed as prime minister in August 1990, Durrani became director general of the ISI.

Long unchallenged, the ISI faced a flurry of court actions in 2012. One court case, dating back to 1996, implicated the ISI in the distribution of $6.5 million through Mehran Bank to a right-wing political alliance in an effort to defeat Bhutto, the incumbent, in the 1990 election. The so-called Mehrangate languished in the Pakistani courts for years until it was refloated by the Supreme Court.[36] Furthermore, after her second government was dismissed in November 1996, Benazir charged that Osama bin Laden had contributed $10 million to the ISI to help in the overthrow of her first government and that the army had terminated her second government following her pledge to crack down on terrorists and radical Islamic groups.

The ISI has continued to play a significant political role in the years following Benazir's death. After the bombing of the Indian embassy in Kabul on July 7, 2008, which killed forty people, including the Indian military attaché, both New Delhi and Washington accused the ISI of complicity. Admiral Mullen and CIA deputy director Stephen Kappes traveled to Islamabad less than a week later to present evidence before General Kayani that linked the ISI with the Taliban forces of Jalaluddin Haqqani in the perpetrating of the bombing. The CIA cut off most intelligence sharing with the ISI, demanding that the ISI be cleaned up and reformed.

A former militant commander revealed in an interview in July 2011 that the ISI and the Pakistani military continue to cultivate and support radical groups. "There are two bodies running these affairs," the former commander declared: "mullahs and retired generals."[37] The charge that the ISI was plagued by "rogue elements" that actively backed radical Islamists is not a new one, according to former ISI chief Asad Durrani: "Twice these vilification campaigns led, under American pressure, to major purges of ISI's rank and file."[38]

The pervasive presence of the ISI and other intelligence agencies in diverse spheres of life in Pakistan, its historical association with Islamist groups that engage in violence, its involvement in past elections in which it influenced outcomes, its systemic practice of unauthorized wiretapping of not only suspected terrorists and other criminals but also politicians, journalists, social activists, and even government officials evidently have undermined the rule of law and distorted civilian-military relations.

These considerations have lent support to the suspicion in Pakistani society, and in the international community, that the ISI, in some shape or form, could have been involved in the assassination of Benazir Bhutto.

WE WILL PROBABLY never know with full certainty who killed Benazir Bhutto, who was behind the planning of the assassination, or who organized and funded the execution of the murder. The list of people and groups that considered Bhutto a hated enemy is long. There are pieces of the murder puzzle but painfully few elements to put them all together.

Some of the wilder theories imagine that Bhutto family members, including her husband, Asif Ali Zardari, or security aides, like Shashenshah, were the killers. But these persons were so close to Bhutto that they would have had numerous and much more propitious and less uncertain occasions to perpetrate such hypothetical assassination. Zardari was in Dubai at the time of the murder; he was unable to control actions at the site of the attack and could not have been responsible, for example, for ordering the hosing down of the crime scene. Most of these hypotheses have no basis in evidence; some do no more than name individuals believed to have benefited in some way from Bhutto's death.

No one believes that the sixteen-year-old suicide bomber who attacked Benazir in Rawalpindi acted alone. The boy was the direct perpetrator, but behind him there were organizers and enablers of the assassination. Al-Qaida had long targeted Benazir and wanted her dead; but it wouldn't have acted without Pakistani support. It seems highly plausible to me that the Pakistani Taliban, including one of its top leaders, Baitullah Mehsud, was among the plotters. They hated Benazir for the mere fact that she was a woman in politics, and they despised her for her democratic values, for her opposition to terrorism, for her "modern Western" upbringing and views, and, in the eyes of the more sectarian, for supposedly being a Shia like her Iranian mother.

But beyond these clear direct culprits and suspects, there are too many loose ends. Several high-ranking police officers were at least criminally negligent and their irresponsible behavior seems attributable to forces above them. It is possible that some rogue elements or fringe agents of the intelligence community may have been involved or have provided logistical support to the assassins, but there is no proof.

Although in her letter sent to General Musharraf on October 16, 2007, Benazir identified people whom she considered a threat to her security (former ISI director general Hamid Gul; the head of the IB retired Brigadier Ijaz Shah; and the then chief minister of Punjab Province Pervaiz Elahi, plus former Sindh chief minister Arbab Ghulam Rahim, named later—all of whom clearly wanted her out of the political landscape), the UN commission did not uncover evidence linking them unequivocally to her murder. However, the police never interrogated the individuals mentioned in Benazir's letter, nor were the individuals invited to meet with the investigators on a voluntary basis. One of them, Hamid Gul, told a reporter that he was rather surprised that the investigators had not questioned him.[39]

Alas, there is no "smoking gun." There were many individuals and organizations interested in seeing Benazir eliminated. Bhutto had emerged as a threat for General Musharraf as she returned to Pakistan to challenge his hold on power, making accusations about election rigging and campaigning in defiance of martial law. Bhutto had sent an e-mail to journalist Wolf Blitzer—through her friend Mark Siegel—that was to be released only if she were killed, which affirmed that she would "hold Musharraf responsible" for her death because she had been "made to feel insecure by his [Musharraf's] minions."[40]

There is evidence that Musharraf was increasingly angry at Benazir for criticizing his regime so severely after having engaged in negotiations to secure a deal with him. In an interview given only days before her death, Musharraf evidenced his acrimony toward Bhutto, complaining that, although there were "many things" he had negotiated with her, those agreements "[had] been violated." Seeming to resent the US and UK pressure to accept Benazir as an ally, Musharraf stated with undisguised sarcasm: "It appears in the West that if a person speaks good English, it's very good. A person who doesn't know good English is quite unpopular in the West. And if he or she happens to be good-looking, then it's better."[41] Some in Musharraf's regime may have felt that Benazir not only had reneged on her promises but also would cause trouble, threaten their hold on power, and even affect the "national interest." But this does not constitute proof of culpability.

General Musharraf certainly bears political and moral responsibility in the assassination, as he did not provide the security that Benazir had so urgently requested and was entitled to receive as a former prime minister, especially considering that she had been the target of a failed assassination attempt in Karachi on the evening of her homecoming on October 18. Moreover, after the Karachi attack, on October 23, senior PPP leader Senator Farooq Naek received a handwritten letter posted from Rawalpindi by a person claiming to be the "head of a team of suicide bombers and friend of Al Qaida" and threatening to assassinate Benazir Bhutto. Naek notified the Supreme Court, urging that the threat be passed on to the government so as to improve Bhutto's security; but according to Naek, the government failed to take proper measures.[42]

During our investigation, we discovered an Interior Ministry letter, dated October 22, 2007, which instructed all provincial governments to provide stringent VVIP-level security to Shaukat Aziz and Chaudhry Shujat Hussain as former prime ministers. The annex to the letter listed specific measures of protection to be implemented by the provincial authorities. Our Commission of Inquiry found it discriminatory and inexcusable that the October 22 directive for ex–prime ministers Aziz and Hussain did not include a similar clear instruction for the protection of Benazir Bhutto, particularly considering that she had been attacked in Karachi just four days prior to the issuance of the letter in question.

The federal government under Musharraf, although fully aware of and tracking the serious threats against Benazir, did little more than pass on those threats to her and notify provincial authorities. The Bhutto team's requests for jammers were met at times, but her security advisers often complained that they did not work properly. Provincial governments provided Bhutto with some security support but only after influential politicians in her party made specific and repeated requests.

A week before Benazir's return to Pakistan on October 18, 2007, three US senators, led by Joe Biden, then chairman of the Senate Foreign Relations Committee, wrote to Musharraf urging him to provide her with "the full level of security support afforded to any former prime minister [including] bomb-proof vehicles and jamming equipment." After Bhutto's assassination Biden declared: "The failure to protect Ms. Bhutto raises a lot of hard questions for the government and security services that must be answered."[43]

"I'll only protect you if you are nice to me," Musharraf allegedly told Bhutto before she returned to Pakistan from her self-imposed exile, according to Ambassador Husain Haqqani.[44] This conversation—reported in greater detail by Ron Suskind in his book *The Way of the World*—took place over the phone from the office of Congressman Tom Lantos, while Benazir was visiting the Capitol. When she asked Musharraf if US officials had talked to him about her security, he replied dismissively that the Americans "could call all they want" about the issue, adding, "You should understand something. Your security is based on the state of *our* relationship."[45]

In Pakistani politics, everything that works is the result of a deal that has been cut. The intelligence agencies and militant groups, for example, have been cutting successful deals in Pakistan for decades. Musharraf and Bhutto had negotiated an inconclusive deal for her return that both parties felt had been violated by the other. Benazir's security was a sort of addendum to the larger agreement that was never negotiated.

The political fingerprints on this case brings to mind the quote "Will no one rid me of this troublesome priest?" which Henry II, king of England, supposedly shouted in frustration at the conduct of the archbishop of Canterbury Thomas Becket, who was subsequently killed by four knights who overheard their king and understood that he wanted Becket dead. In Benazir's case, there was more than a single power figure who wished to be rid of that "troublesome" woman.

Benazir's murder reminds me of the Spanish play *Fuente Ovejuna*, in which the hated ruler of the village Fuente Ovejuna is killed and the magistrate who investigates the crime cannot find the culprit. During the investigation, every villager interrogated declares that Fuente Ovejuna did it. In Benazir's case too, it would seem that the village assassinated her: Al-Qaida gave the order; the Pakistani Taliban executed the attack, possibly backed or at least encouraged by elements of the Establishment; the Musharraf government facilitated the crime by not providing her with adequate security; local senior policemen attempted a cover-up; Benazir's lead security team failed to properly safeguard her; and most Pakistani political actors would rather turn the page than continue investigating who was behind her assassination.

PROBABLY NO GOVERNMENT will be able or willing to fully disentangle the truth from the complex web of implication in Benazir Bhutto's assassination. In a sense, Pakistani ambassador to the UN Abdullah Haroon was right when he was quoted as saying that Pakistan was unlikely to take steps to address the security and judicial failures detailed in the commission's report and that the country's history showed that "nothing is ever taken to conclusion."[46] It may well be that Benazir Bhutto's assassination will be another unresolved case in the long history of impunity in Pakistan and that the controversy surrounding her assassination will endure as much as her memory.

The author delivering the final report on the assassination of Benazir Bhutto to UN Secretary-General Ban Ki-moon on April 15, 2010. Secretary-General Ban then handed over the report to the permanent representative of Pakistan to the United Nations, Ambassador Abdullah Hussain Haroon.

9

The Investigation's Repercussions

In early May 2010, my wife, Pamela, and I were waiting for a subway train at East Fifty-Ninth Street and Lexington Avenue in New York City. Among the crowd was a man who paced up and down the platform, looking at me inquisitively. He seemed South American, I thought. At times, compatriots on vacation in the city have recognized me as a former Chilean authority. But this man did not look like a tourist. Eventually he approached me.

"Are you Ambassador Muñoz of Chile?" he asked.

"Yes, I am," I replied.

"I'm Pakistani. You are the most wanted person in Pakistan," the man said.

I was shocked. This was a situation I never expected to encounter in the Manhattan subway.

"I am most wanted in a positive or negative sense?" I managed to ask.

"Positively," he answered. "I sometimes contribute to an electronic media outlet in Pakistan, so I know who you are. I've seen you on TV and other media these days. You made a great contribution to establish the truth on Benazir's death. But," he continued, "nothing will happen. Your contribution will be wasted and lost."

I thanked the Pakistani, and my wife and I moved toward the train as it approached the station.

I had delivered the report formally to Secretary-General Ban Ki-moon at a brief ceremony, accompanied by colleague commissioner Marzuki Darusman. Our other colleague, Peter Fitzgerald, had not been able to travel from Ireland. The secretary-general handed the report to the Pakistani ambassador to the UN, Abdullah Haroon, who received it on behalf of his government. After the ceremony, Marzuki and I gave a press conference, broadcast live on the Internet, to a pressroom packed with about one hundred journalists from around the world.

Efforts by the government of Pakistan and other interested parties to gain advance access to our report had been denied, as we had kept it under tight control until it was delivered to the secretary-general.

US and other Western media portrayed the report in a positive light. The *Guardian* quoted a spokesperson of Human Rights Watch who expressed hope that the report would "contribute to halting the impunity with which Pakistan's intelligence agencies and non-state actors perpetrate abuses, including political assassination," adding that regarding Benazir Bhutto's assassination, the report "is the closest we'll get"[1] to the truth. According to the *Guardian*, the UN report had become a "watershed in moribund efforts to solve the mystery of Bhutto's death."[2] The *New York Times* asserted that although the report did not uncover who killed Benazir, it "did put its finger on what remains the most troubling part of Pakistan's reality, the dominance of its military and intelligence services over civilian leaders." The article added that "some in Pakistan expressed delight" at the findings, saying the exposure "would force an uncomfortable conversation in Pakistan."[3] The *Economist* characterized our document as "a high-powered U.N. report," adding that it had "highlighted the debilitating effect on Pakistan's institutions of its pervasive spells of military rule."[4]

In Pakistan, the reactions to the report got entangled with domestic politics. The evaluations depended on whether the commentators were pro-government or of the opposition; pundits cherry-picked portions of the report to either blast Musharraf or Zardari and other government officials or simply to disparage the commissioners, particularly me as chairman of the Commission of Inquiry. Most editorials and columnists praised the report as a serious contribution toward establishing the truth and for having raised pertinent questions about issues of governance, civil-military relations, and the state of the political and judicial institutions of the country. Many comments underlined the obvious: that the commission had failed to identify the culprits of Bhutto's murder—a responsibility beyond our mandate.

Some particularly negative comments seemed tainted by spin from intelligence agencies—like the unfounded assertion that the commission had cost Pakistan $100 million. Former director general of the ISI Hamid Gul—who refused to be interviewed by the commission—following a conventional spy's script, attempted to deflect attention to others by characterizing the document as a "save Zardari" report. Gul affirmed that he did not believe that Al-Qaida and the Taliban were involved in the murder and insinuated a US responsibility by indicating that there was no mention in the report of "the United States and Blackwater, despite the fact that Benazir Bhutto had deviated from the American agenda before her assassination."[5]

A spokesperson for General Pervez Musharraf called the UN

report "a pack of lies" based on rumors, enigmatically noting that Musharraf believed he had "one final bullet in his pistol which he will use for his defense in the case." The spokesperson blamed Benazir Bhutto for her assassination, for having "exposed herself to the attacker," and criticized me personally by saying I was "no Sherlock Holmes."[6]

One writer denounced me by pointing out that during the 1973 military coup against the government of President Salvador Allende, I had handled explosives and other weapons in a youthful attempt at resistance.[7] (I wrote about this in my book *The Dictator's Shadow*.) How, asked the essayist, could a terrorist be in charge of investigating a terrorist bombing? But another blogger, mentioning my same background of resistance against a dictatorship, defended the report.[8]

The reaction of the Pakistani authorities was hesitant and unclear. They seemed genuinely surprised by the detailed analysis, evidence, and recommendations of the report that emanated from the 250 interviews we had conducted; the review of hundreds of documents, videos, photographs, and other documentary materials; and the meetings with Pakistani officials, private citizens, diplomats, and people with knowledge relevant to our investigation.

One of the government's first reactions came from Farhatullah Babar, spokesperson for President Zardari, who stated that the PPP welcomed the report and announced that persons, including ex-president Pervez Musharraf, named "for negligence or complicity in the conspiracy" would be "investigated and cases also brought against them in light of legal opinion."[9]

A special meeting on a Saturday night at the president's residence to discuss the report—steered by Zardari himself and in the presence of Prime Minister Gilani—"accepted the report findings and observations" and also "thanked the U.N. Commission of Inquiry for its efforts."[10] Farahnaz Ispahani, a Zardari aide, stated that the report would "pave the way for a proper police investigation and possible penal procedures."[11] Ambassador Abdullah Hussain Haroon, Pakistan's permanent representative to the UN, described the report as "a very clean factual picture that was well conceived, well written and well intentioned." He added that it gave "the solid foundation and the backing of the international community for the criminal matter now to be raised and taken to its final conclusion."[12]

President Zardari declared that the UN report had confirmed the apprehensions of the PPP about the assassination of Benazir Bhutto.[13] Later on, Zardari added that the report had "strengthened the hands of the government to vigorously pursue the investigations and to bring the culprits to justice."[14]

Despite the positive reactions to the report from governmental sources, rumors indicated that there was dissatisfaction in some official quarters. Two months after the report had been released, the Pakistani government, through the foreign minister, sent an official note to UN secretary-general Ban Ki-moon, on June 14, 2010, complaining that the commission should have extended its work to access intelligence from third-party states, objecting that the report lacked "source attribution" and exhibited "undue confidentiality" regarding the names of persons interviewed and sources of information and raising methodological questions about the inquiry. The letter expressed dissatisfaction at the "disproportionate space" dedicated in the report to Pakistan's army, the intelligence agencies, and the Establishment.

The June 14 letter questioning the work of the Commission of Inquiry was soon leaked to the Pakistani media.[15] UN secretary-general Ban Ki-moon responded by fully endorsing the work of the commission. Through his spokesperson Farhan Haq, the secretary-general affirmed that "the report painstakingly sets out the facts regarding the assassination and provides an extensive description of the circumstances around the crime." The declaration by the spokesperson went on to state that "the secretary-general has full confidence in the Commission's judgment. He believes that the report produced by the Commission speaks for itself and can be helpful to any subsequent investigation. The work of the Commission is complete. The secretary-general stands by the report."[16]

The secretary-general's solid backing of our work placed the Pakistani government in an awkward position. According to press stories, Islamabad instructed Ambassador Abdullah Haroon "to urge the world body to tone down its reply over Foreign Minister Shah Mehmood Qureshi's letter in which he had criticized the U.N. Inquiry Commission." The Pakistani government, according to one source, feared "a tough response from U.N. Secretary-General Ban Ki-moon."[17] One press version erroneously attributed to me the authorship of the secretary-general's letter, "kept secret," according to the news agency, by the Pakistani government and described as "strongly worded."[18] In fact, I learned about the existence of said letter through the media.

A few months later, *Dawn* newspaper revealed that the government's objections to the report had been driven by the army, which had prepared a reply presented to the prime minister and channeled through the foreign minister. "Major-General Athar Abbas acknowledged that the military had some reservations on the report because it went beyond the mandate of the U.N. Commission," it was reported.[19] Another news story indicated that Islamabad was disgruntled at the finger-pointing at the security services and at the role of leaders like Rehman Malik and Babar Awan.

The backdrop to such surprising developments was that a few weeks before the release of the report, the Islamabad government, driven by Minister of the Interior Rehman Malik, had requested an extension of the commission's mandate so that it could gather intelligence on the murder allegedly held by friendly neighboring countries. The move was, in our opinion, an effort to create excuses to attack the report in case the commission chose not to follow the advice to consult those intelligence sources.

The mandate of the commission had been already extended once. After a deteriorating security situation in Pakistan caused us to cancel a visit to the country in November 2009, Secretary-General Ban Ki-moon authorized an extension beyond the planned December 31, 2009, conclusion. Secretary-General Ban gave us another three months, up to March 31, 2010. This new and unsolicited extension suggested by the government of Pakistan was at best a delaying tactic and at worst a political play.

On March 29 at 5:30 p.m., New York time, I received a phone call from Minister Rehman Malik informing me that President Zardari had signed a letter asking the secretary-general for an extension of the mandate, even though we had communicated to Islamabad that such an extension was unnecessary, as we had all the information we required; the report was finished, except for some final editorial touches. Malik told me that actually, the Zardari letter would be replaced by a letter from him as minister of the interior to me as chairman of the commission requesting that I convey the request in question to Secretary-General Ban.

Malik stressed that there was important information to be obtained from Afghan president Hamid Karzai regarding the threats to Benazir Bhutto. At the same time, he informed me that the Islamabad government was sending agents to interview the head of Afghan intelligence on the matter. "There is an Egyptian involved," Malik told me.

I reminded Minister Malik that our inquiry was into the facts and circumstances of the assassination and that identifying culprits was beyond our mandate. I asked again why this information hadn't been communicated to us before, since evidently the government must have known about this intelligence from "brotherly countries." Malik insisted on the importance of interviewing President Karzai, the United Arab Emirates intelligence authorities, and, he added, Condoleezza Rice. I let him know that former secretary Rice had declined to speak to the commission and that, in any case, we had interviewed her key assistant Richard Boucher.

Malik asked for an extension of ten days, instead of the one month requested in the Zardari letter and the nine-month extension Malik had originally suggested.

The following day, Pakistani ambassador Abdullah Haroon contacted me at 9:25 a.m. to tell me that he had "instructions" to deliver the letter signed by President Zardari to the secretary-general. Personally, he confessed, he felt our work was done and that the extension was unnecessary. That same day, the secretary-general issued a statement accepting "an urgent request by the President of Pakistan to delay the presentation of the report" until April 15, 2010. The statement added, "The Commission has informed the secretary-general that, as of today, all relevant facts and circumstances have been explored, and the report is complete and ready to be delivered."[20] This was a most unusual and awkward situation. The secretary-general agreed to delay the release of a report that was already completed, for what Pakistan considered was necessary additional time for information gathering that was deemed unnecessary by the commissioners.

As we expected, the Pakistani press reported that the extension had been requested so that the report could gain "more credibility" by including inputs from Afghanistan, the United Arab Emirates and Saudi Arabia about the death threats Benazir Bhutto was facing as she returned to Pakistan from her voluntary exile in 2007.[21] One article suggested that the purpose of the delay was "to avert the possible criticism some key position holders within Pakistan's corridors of power are likely to face in the wake of the publication of the U.N. Commission findings, by keeping the issue lingering."[22]

Abundant news reports from US and international media speculated about the contents of the report, but the commission had avoided leaks assiduously. Mark Siegel, acting on behalf of the Zardari government, phoned one of our team members to ask if the Pakistani president could see the report before it was released. With due courtesy, we turned him down. In fact, Secretary-General Ban Ki-moon and his executive team learned of the contents of the commission's report only on the morning of April 15 when we delivered it to him during a brief ceremony in his office.

Coinciding with the postponement of the delivery of our report, the resident coordinator of the United Nations system in Pakistan announced he had decided to order the closing of all UN offices throughout the country for three days and directed staff "to avoid travelling or exposing themselves in public during this period,"[23] as a security measure. Local newspapers widely covered the representative's decision and the police informed that the necessary arrangements were being made. We also learned that the UN representative had stated that the substance of our report would be damaging to the organization's role in Pakistan, even though he knew nothing about its contents. My fellow commissioners and I were irate, and we communicated our distress to the proper UN authorities in New York.

A few days before the Pakistani government's request to extend the mandate of the commission, I had written a letter on behalf of the commissioners to Minister Malik reminding him that we had "repeatedly attempted to secure direct interviews with the competent authorities of the United Arab Emirates (UAE), Saudi Arabia and Afghanistan to ascertain information that they conveyed to Ms. Bhutto regarding threats on her life." But, we reminded Malik, those requests had not been accommodated. However, since the Pakistani government had detailed information on the death threats, we requested confirmation of the data we had gathered about them. We never received a response to that letter.

US sources confirmed to the commission that much of the information on death-threat warnings communicated by friendly countries, particularly the UAE, actually had originated from the Pakistani government. After 9/11, the ISI and the CIA had developed "Project Z," a massive database project to track terrorist groups, which included software to intercept communications. Such work had detected militant cells that were following Benazir. Considering that the former prime minister did not trust the Musharraf government, conveying information from foreign sources seemed more credible.[24]

Our commission was told by present and former senior officials of the ISI that they had received intelligence regarding threats to Bhutto from representatives of the governments of Saudi Arabia and the United Arab Emirates. UAE officials confirmed to the commission that government-to-government information sharing had occurred. The ISI officials told us that on at least two occasions, representatives from both countries flew to Pakistan to provide this and other information, which generally coincided with their own.

Minister Rehman Malik told the commission that he had received information from a "brotherly country" about another significant threat aimed at Bhutto and himself. Malik did not specify the details of the threat, despite our request. Almost two years after our report was issued, the Pakistani press revealed that a letter had been sent by the ISI to then secretary of the interior Kamal Shah seventeen days before Bhutto's assassination, warning that "a few extremist groups related to Al-Qaida have made some plan to assassinate Mrs. Benazir Bhutto and her adviser Rehman Malik on 21 December, 2007." The brief message, transmitted later to Malik, ended saying, "The exact plan of execution not known."[25]

Our communications with the authorities in Afghanistan and the UAE did not yield any new information relevant to the report. An interview by a member of our team with intelligence authorities from the UAE in Dubai in March 2010 did not produce anything different from what we already knew. And we were told repeatedly by Kabul authorities, through the Afghan Mission to the UN, that the officials present during the conversation between President Karzai and Benazir Bhutto on the morning of her assassination did not possess any specific information to share with us. In fact, a news story in *Dawn* affirmed that the Pakistani agents conducting the so-called second FIA investigation into Benazir's murder had contacted the Afghan government about the threats on her life but that the Afghan foreign ministry had declared that "it had no record which suggested that President Karzai had informed Benazir about a possible threat to her life."[26] Interestingly, the same *Dawn* story reported that during their inquiry, the FIA investigators had been unable to interview high military officers and that when they had tried to contact General Musharraf, Interior Minister Rehman Malik had stopped them, explaining that the government "had some kind of deal" with the former ruler.[27]

THE COMMISSION'S REPORT did have some significant political and judicial repercussions. Four days after the release of the report, the Pakistani government went into action and suspended eight officials who had been responsible for Bhutto's security at Liaquat Bagh, including Rawalpindi police chief Saud Aziz. Presidential spokesperson Farhatullah Babar announced the suspension of the officials and their inclusion on an exit control list barring them from leaving the country. Retired brigadier Javed Iqbal Cheema's contract as director general for civil defense was canceled, and he was also placed on the exit control list. A few days later, on April 24, the government constituted a three-member fact-finding committee led by Cabinet Secretary Abdul Rauf to investigate the issue of the washing of the crime scene where Bhutto had been assassinated. In parallel, the FIA of Pakistan also began an inquiry. But less than a month later, the three-member committee cleared those identified in the report as responsible for hosing down the crime scene—a decision that the Pakistani press called a "trashing of the U.N. report."[28]

The Rawalpindi police officials defended their washing of the crime scene with some peculiar arguments. "Nobody has asked the question: what evidence was lost by washing the scene?" said Police Chief Saud Aziz. "We assembled twenty-three pieces," he reasoned, meaning that "nothing was lost by washing of the crime site."[29]

Minister Rehman Malik, during an interview outside the Lahore High Court shortly after the release of our report, declared that "the real killers of former Prime Minister Benazir Bhutto were not exposed in the report issued by the United Nations Inquiry Commission."[30] It was a rather surprising statement coming from the commission's contact person in the Pakistani government who knew very well that the commission's role was not to expose any culprits of the crime. In mid-2011 Malik affirmed that Osama bin Laden was involved in the murder of the former prime minister, without elaborating any further.[31] Later, in December 2012, Minister Malik announced that he would reveal Benazir Bhutto's killers in a forthcoming book.[32]

President Zardari seemed to suggest that Taliban or Al-Qaida terrorists along with members of the Establishment had perpetrated the murder of his wife when, addressing a jirga at the Governor's House in Peshawar, he asserted that "those who were granted refuge 30 years ago" had killed Bhutto, adding that people in the provinces needed to "check that their neighbors were not illegal foreigners or were involved in unlawful activities."[33]

In a surprising development, Pakistan's federal defense production minister resigned after a controversy erupted when he accused the army of killing several high-profile Pakistani figures, including Benazir Bhutto. Abdul Qayyum Khan Jatoi stated during a televised press conference in Quetta, "We provided the army with uniforms and boots not so that they kill their own fellow countrymen, kill Nawab Sahib Bugti and Benazir Bhutto."[34] Nothing much came of Jatoi's denunciations after his dismissal, as he did not provide any details for his broad accusations.

An antiterrorist court in Rawalpindi took the UN report seriously and conducted detailed interrogations of the police officers in charge of Bhutto's protection. Prosecutor Chaudhry Zulfikar Ali told the media that former police chief Saud Aziz and former deputy police chief Khurram Shahzad had named four MI and ISI officials of major and colonel rank levels who had been in contact with them after Bhutto's murder.[35] The two former police officers were arrested in December 2010 by the FIA after the antiterrorist court revoked their bail. The prosecutor explained that Aziz and Shahzad "were responsible for Bhutto's security. They ordered the crime scene to be hosed down despite resistance from other officials."[36] The prosecutor added that it was the police officers' "duty to carry out the post-mortem" examination of the former prime minister.[37]

Shortly thereafter, in February 2011, the same Rawalpindi court issued a subpoena for the arrest of former president Musharraf, then living in voluntary exile in London, for failing to provide adequate security to Bhutto before and during the rally and for not having passed to competent authorities the information available about Taliban plans to assassinate her. Prosecutor Zulfikar Ali added that former police officers Aziz and Shahzad had declared that they had removed the security detail for Benazir Bhutto, just before she departed the venue where she was speaking, on the orders of Musharraf.[38] Prosecutor Zulfikar Ali revealed that the court had tried to contact Musharraf at his London address and that a list of questions had been sent to him several months ago, but he had refused to answer the queries.

Adding to the mystery surrounding the Bhutto case, state prosecutor Zulfikar Ali was assassinated on May 3, 2013, by gunmen who riddled his vehicle with bullets as he drove to work to a hearing on the Bhutto case. Zulfikar Ali was hit by thirteen bullets by unknown assailants. Some security experts declared that the prosecutor was "a marked man because he had been prosecuting militants who were jailed in connection with Bhutto's death"[39] and other terrorism trials.

Regarding the arrest warrant issued by the court against General Musharraf, his spokesperson, Fawad Chaudhry, characterized it as "totally ridiculous." He then added, "How can the president of a country be made responsible for the non-provision of security? It's totally ridiculous. You cannot pin criminal responsibility on a president for that."[40] Chaudhry had conveniently ignored Musharraf's stern warning to Bhutto: "Your security is based on the state of our relationship."

In parallel, rumors abounded in Pakistan that more suspects in the Bhutto crime were being arrested. Interior Minister Rehman Malik admitted that more suspects involved in the assassination had indeed been arrested. The Ministry of the Interior had supposedly identified nine coconspirators of which five were still alive. The five were the ones who allegedly hired the killers and gave them shelter and logistical support. The assassination plot was hatched in the formal residence of an army brigadier, according to the official investigation report.[41]

In November 2011, the antiterrorist court charged former police chief Saud Aziz and former deputy police chief Khurram Shahzad, along with five militants believed to be members of the Pakistani Taliban, with criminal conspiracy and murder. Of the five militants, under arrest since 2007, two of them admitted to helping in the suicide bombing. Aziz and Shahzad returned to jail after they had been freed on bail following their initial arrest in December 2010.[42]

Meanwhile, in August 2011, Special Judge Shahid Rafique of the antiterrorist court conducting the Bhutto case ordered Pakistani authorities to seize all of Pervez Musharraf's assets, following his failure to appear before the court. Musharraf's property details provided by the court to the FIA included a farmhouse, a plot of land, and deposits in six different banks.

In February 2012, Minister Malik presented, during a briefing to the Sindh Assembly, the much-awaited "final investigation report" of the official inquiry into Bhutto's assassination, conducted by the FIA. Using audio and video footage, Minister Malik revealed that twenty-seven terrorist groups were responsible for having executed the murder, including Baitullah Mehsud, the Haqqani network, and the banned Tehrik-i-Taliban Pakistan. Malik admitted that the planners of the crime were still at large and that more time was needed to collect further evidence. He added that thirteen suspects were being prosecuted; he also accused former president Pervez Musharraf of not providing adequate security to Benazir Bhutto and announced that a request would be made to Interpol for his arrest.[43] The report also accused police officers Saud Aziz and Khurram Shahzad of being part of the conspiracy to kill Bhutto.[44]

Musharraf canceled plans to return to Pakistan in January 2012 to campaign for upcoming parliamentary elections after he was warned he would face immediate arrest. Months later, Musharraf shrugged off Pakistan's call for Interpol to arrest him, reiterating that he would return "of his own accord" and criticized the current government, cautioning that "people are again running to the military to save the country."[45] Musharraf finally arrived back in Pakistan on March 24, 2013, greeted by what a newspaper described as "threats and small crowds."[46] Local media indicated that barely days after his return to Pakistan General Musharraf was facing "one petition after another being moved against him in the Supreme Court"[47] and other tribunals, including over the Bhutto case. In fact, in late April 2013, the Rawalpindi anti-terrorism court placed Musharraf on a judicial remand for charges of failing to provide adequate security to Bhutto prior to her assassination.

On the fifth anniversary of Benazir Bhutto's murder, *Dawn* newspaper summarized a widespread sense of frustration with the judicial investigations into the assassination: "Repeated and unending investigations, indifferent lawyers, a chaotic judicial system and a government that really didn't care, have all ensured that Benazir Bhutto's trial is going nowhere."[48] The fifth anniversary of the assassination was marked, instead, by the launching of the political career of Bilawal Bhutto Zardari, son of the former prime minister and of President Zardari, and chairman of the PPP, who delivered his first major public speech before two hundred thousand people gathered at the Bhutto family mausoleum. "We are messengers of peace and stand by democracy, and we are afraid neither of any terrorist nor any dictator,"[49] said Bilawal, who had just completed his Oxford education and was now the fourth generation of his family to enter politics.

EPILOGUE

EPILOGUE

Reflections on Bhutto, bin Laden, and Pakistan's Ties to the United States

IN MID-AUGUST 1996, the CIA gained intelligence that Osama bin Laden and his top lieutenants were planning a meeting in one of his Afghanistan camps on August 20. President Bill Clinton's administration had been tracking bin Laden and saw this as an opportunity to retaliate for the bombings against the US embassies in Kenya and Tanzania. But launching air strikes against bin Laden involved flying over Pakistani airspace.

Clinton knew that the ISI used some of the same camps that bin Laden and Al-Qaida did to train the Taliban and insurgents who fought in Kashmir. If the White House informed Pakistani authorities about the planned attacks in advance, the intelligence services surely would warn the Taliban or even Al-Qaida, Clinton reasoned. If the US government didn't tell Islamabad, it could cause bilateral tension and, moreover, the Pakistanis could mistakenly assume that the flying missiles had been launched at them by India and retaliate—conceivably even with nuclear weapons.

President Clinton instructed the vice chairman of the Joint

Chiefs of Staff, General Joe Ralston, to have dinner with the top Pakistani military commander at the precise time of the scheduled raids so as to tell him about the operation only minutes before the missiles entered Pakistani airspace, "too late to alert the Taliban or Al Qaida, but in time to avoid having them shot down or sparking a counter attack on India."[1] The operation went through well enough as far as Pakistan was concerned, but bin Laden escaped.

Getting Osama bin Laden became a security priority for Clinton. In July 1999, with the support of then prime minister Nawaz Sharif, the CIA began to train sixty Pakistani troops as commandos to penetrate Afghanistan in search of bin Laden. The president was skeptical about the project because even with Sharif's cooperation, the Pakistani military and the ISI were full of Taliban and Al-Qaida sympathizers who could foil the operation. But Clinton thought it was worth trying. When Nawaz Sharif was overthrown in a military coup by General Pervez Musharraf on October 12, 1999, the project to send the Pakistani commandos into Afghanistan to capture or kill bin Laden was aborted.[2]

Washington had been growing increasingly impatient and frustrated with the Pakistani army's reluctance to capture Osama bin Laden and other Al-Qaida leaders known to reside in Pakistani territory. Mullah Omar, the Afghan Taliban commander, had been living in Quetta since 2002, accommodated by the ISI in safe houses run by the Jamiat Ulema-e-Islam party, which had come to power in the Quetta provincial government. Abu Zubaydah, a senior Al-Qaida recruiter, had been living openly in Peshawar since 1997, running a guesthouse known as the House of Martyrs before he was captured near Lahore on March 28, 2002. The Clinton administration had repeatedly asked President Musharraf to extradite Zubaydah, but the ISI denied knowing his whereabouts, despite the fact that he had worked for the ISI before 9/11.[3] Much later, during the George W. Bush administration, US ambassador to Afghanistan Zalmay Khalilzad expressed frustration with such situations and complained: "[Mullah Akhtar] Usmani, who is one of the Taliban leaders, spoke to Pakistan's Geo TV at a time when the Pakistani intelligence service claimed that they did not know where [he was]."[4] In another incident, in June 2011, the Pakistani army denied that its security forces had tipped off insurgents at bomb-making factories in the tribal belt after the United States had shared satellite information with Pakistan. According to US sources, within twenty-four hours of sharing the information, the militants cleared out the bomb-making sites.[5]

President George W. Bush trusted his friend General Musharraf to hunt and capture Osama bin Laden. During a White House visit by Musharraf in September 2006, Bush declared: "When the President [Musharraf] looks me in the eye and says . . . 'if we find—when we find Usama bin Laden, he will be brought to justice' I believe him. And we'll let the tactics speak for themselves after it happens."[6]

A sign of change in US tolerance toward Pakistani leaks occurred on September 3, 2008, when helicopters transporting US Navy SEALs landed near Angur Adda in South Waziristan on a first-ever-acknowledged ground attack on Pakistani soil. The operation killed twenty-five militants.[7] A few days later, on September 19, the chief of army staff General Kayani flew to meet US chairman of the Joint Chiefs of Staff Mike Mullen aboard the aircraft carrier USS *Abraham Lincoln*, where Kayani told his US counterpart that dire consequences would follow another such invasion of Pakistani territory.

The Barack Obama administration had to weigh these concerns before launching further attacks. There were plenty of targets to go after, but it had to consider the impact within Pakistan—the potential for an anti-American reaction by the public, the political elite, and particularly the army. Then again, unilateral attacks had proven effective as a deterrent to jihadists threatening US troops in Afghanistan or planning terrorist operations against American interests worldwide, including on US soil.

By the time Osama bin Laden was killed on Sunday, May 1, 2011, in his residence in Abbottabad, home to Pakistani's leading military academy and a nuclear-weapons site, the terrorist chief was in his sixth year of residence in the city's Bilal Town neighborhood, a middle-class sector less than a mile from the entrance to the academy. Most US Predator drone strikes seeking to kill bin Laden and his Al-Qaida aides concentrated in the Pakistani's tribal regions, some two hundred miles away to the west.

Already during the 2008 presidential election debates, Barack Obama had expressed his determination to pursue Osama bin Laden into Pakistan if Islamabad was "unable or unwilling" to eliminate him and other Al-Qaida leaders. After his election, President Obama intensified the CIA's classified drone program: during his first year in office, there were more missile strikes inside Pakistan than in all of President Bush's years in office combined.

After the White House received solid intelligence that bin Laden was living in the compound at Abbottabad, and after President Obama had taken the decision to authorize the Navy SEAL operation—against the advice of his top national security team—he faced a similar dilemma to the one President Clinton had confronted in 1996 when he decided to fire missiles at an Osama bin Laden camp over Pakistani airspace: whether to inform the Pakistanis in advance about the impending attack, so as not to damage an already-tense bilateral relationship, or to keep them out of the loop to ensure that bin Laden would not be warned by Pakistani intelligence to evacuate.

According to a report,[8] early in the process President Obama ruled out a joint operation with Pakistan. Did bin Laden have protectors in the intelligence establishment or higher up in the army hierarchy? The tight circle around Obama did not know the answer, which prompted a decision to maintain full secrecy. In the end, only when the US helicopters had escaped Pakistani airspace did Obama authorize Admiral Mike Mullen, the chairman of the Joint Chiefs of Staff, to phone General Kayani, Pakistan's chief of army staff, the next day around 3:00 a.m. local time to tell him about the raid.

SEAL teams had surreptitiously entered Pakistan on ten to twelve previous occasions before the bin Laden operation. Most of those attacks by SEALs from the Naval Special Warfare Development Group and by Green Berets were forays into North and South Waziristan, including the widely reported raid at Angur Adda in September 2008. Abbottabad was the farthest the special US team had ventured into Pakistani territory.[9]

General Kayani reportedly was stunned. Did the Pakistanis know that bin Laden was hiding in Abbottabad, meaning that the military leadership was complicit in harboring him? Or did the Pakistanis simply not know that the United States' most wanted man was living for six years in their territory along with his wives, children, and aides? No firm evidence suggests that the Pakistani military and intelligence establishment knew of bin Laden's whereabouts. My guess is that this was more than an intelligence failure on the part of the Pakistanis; they simply did not look hard enough for bin Laden. But in reality, no matter how they dealt with the Al-Qaida leader, they were bound to lose in some way: if they kept his location secret from the Americans, it would have endangered the bilateral relationship on a critical issue for the US government and people, but if they located him, arrested him, and handed him over to the US government, it would have provoked the ire of significant sectors of the Pakistani population and the "Muslim street."

It cannot be ruled out that the Section S, which works closely with Taliban and Al-Qaida militants, or other elements of the ISI, might have known about bin Laden's whereabouts. It is possible that high-level intelligence authorities and army chiefs turned a blind eye. Knowing too much about thorny issues can be a problem. What is clear is that bin Laden had some kind of Pakistani support structure that allowed him to spend nine years on the run in Pakistan after 9/11, changing houses up to seven times in Swat, Haripur, and Abbottabad, and possibly even undergoing a kidney transplant operation in 2002. Given bin Laden's paranoia regarding security matters, it is unlikely that he would have put his personal safety in the hands of the Pakistani military, despite some indications that at some point, he and his aides discussed cutting a deal with Pakistani officials that involved Al-Qaida refraining from attacking targets within the country in exchange for protection.[10]

In July 2013, Al Jazeera revealed on its website a 336-page report of the Abbottabad Commission that concluded that Osama bin Laden's nine-year-long stay in Pakistan and the May 2011 US Navy SEALs raid in which he was killed, were undetected due to "gross incompetence" of the state institutions, including, particularly, the ISI. The five-member commission led by Justice Javed Iqbal asserted in its report that "culpable negligence and incompetence at almost all levels of government can more or less be conclusively established."[11]

Pakistanis very likely want to forget about the bin Laden raid episode, as well as the official commission of inquiry, led by a Supreme Court judge, that was set up to look into the operation. That's why on the night of February 25, 2012, authorities in Abbottabad sent bulldozers to completely demolish bin Laden's house, as if to erase it from collective memory. Pakistani military officials arrested at least five Pakistanis for assisting the CIA in the bin Laden raid, including physician Shakil Afridi, who had run a fake vaccination program as a ruse to gain DNA evidence from the bin Laden family—which he did not get. The doctor's imprisonment angered US authorities.[12]

But the US government also had reason to put the bin Laden raid behind it, especially regarding the issue of the hypothetical support that the Al-Qaida leader might have received from the security establishment. Washington's relations with Islamabad are too crucial to risk an all-out break, even if Pakistani officials did know about bin Laden's whereabouts. Neither the United States nor Pakistan can afford a complete breakdown of bilateral relations.

Both Benazir's and Osama's killings reveal the profound mistrust and contradictions that have characterized US-Pakistan ties in recent history. The US government could not reveal the bin Laden operation to its Pakistani counterpart because Islamabad, guarding its own interests, has played and will continue to play a double game of cooperation with Washington and support of the Taliban. At times, the Pakistan army and the ISI will capture or even kill some Taliban or Al-Qaida operatives for concrete security reasons or to satisfy American pressures, but it preserves and protects the Taliban because it is a force by which to gain strategic depth in Afghanistan and a defense mechanism against India. The Pakistani government will probably free from jail and/or spare the "good Taliban" who do not turn their guns on the Pakistani state and are willing to engage in peace talks, and target for elimination those who fight the army and who could become a threat to national security in the long run.

After all, Pakistanis know well that the Americans embraced jihadists, like Osama bin Laden, when Washington's priority was to defeat the Soviets in Afghanistan. Likewise, the Pakistanis have fashioned their own relationship with the jihadists. After 9/11, the US government wanted Benazir in power to favor democratic reforms and secularism, but because of the so-called war on terror, it also needed General Musharraf and the ISI. Washington wanted change in Pakistan but enough stability to rein in the Taliban and Al-Qaida and to ensure the safe control of Pakistan's nuclear arsenal.

The United States and Pakistan are condemned to live with each other. The severe blows that assailed the partnership during its annus horribilis—2011—underscored the endurance of the bilateral relationship.

After the Navy SEAL team killed bin Laden in Abbottabad in May, Parliament and the press heaped withering criticism on the United States and on General Kayani for the violation of Pakistani sovereignty. But this was not the first such incident that year, as 2011 had started inauspiciously when on January 27, Raymond Davis, a CIA operative involved in a covert operation to penetrate the Lashkar-e-Taiba militant group, killed two men during what he claimed was a robbery attempt, leading to his arrest by the Pakistani police. Heavy negotiations resulted in his release after a period of detention, but Washington was forced to cut a substantial part of its Special Operations Forces on Pakistani soil and withdraw all CIA contractors.[13]

Before the raid on bin Laden's hideout, a White House report had criticized Pakistan's efforts to defeat Al-Qaida and associated militants "despite the unprecedented and sustained deployment of over 147,000 forces and the deaths of 2,575 Pakistani troops since 2001." The report held that Pakistan's poor planning for the "hold and build" stages of its military operations was enabling militants to return to areas from which they had been driven.[14] A visit by Senator John Kerry to Islamabad a few days after the bin Laden raid cooled tempers for a while in early summer, until renewed drone attacks rekindled the anti-American clamor. Relations entered crisis mode once again in September when Haqqani militants marked the tenth anniversary of 9/11 by attacking American soldiers with a truck bomb in Afghanistan's Wardak Province, wounding seventy-seven US troops, and launching a twenty-hour rocket-propelled grenade attack on the US embassy in Kabul. Two days later, on Capitol Hill, Admiral Mike Mullen, the outgoing chairman of the Joint Chiefs of Staff—who had cultivated a personal relationship with General Kayani—told US congressmen that the Haqqani network "acts as a veritable arm of Pakistan's Inter-Services Intelligence agency,"[15] thus linking the ISI to the Haqqani attack on the US embassy in Kabul.

Mullen's declarations caused great alarm in Islamabad, as some feared an all-out US invasion of Pakistan and/or an American attempt to capture its prized nuclear arsenal. Military leaders and politicians representing thirty-two political parties gathered at the residence of Prime Minister Yousuf Raza Gilani on September 29 to discuss Mullen's charges. The political leaders issued a thirteen-point declaration affirming that Admiral Mullen's statements were "without substance and derogatory to a partnership approach."[16]

A week later, President Obama, at a Washington press conference, warned that the United States would not "feel comfortable with a long-term strategic relationship with Pakistan if we don't think that they're mindful of our interests as well."[17] Two weeks after Obama's statement, Secretary of State Hillary Rodham Clinton, leading a high-level US delegation to Islamabad, told Pakistani prime minister Gilani and military authorities that the United States would act unilaterally, if necessary, to attack militant forces that use Pakistani territory as a haven to launch operations to kill Americans.

The controversy known as "memogate" shook bilateral relations when it was revealed that supposedly, the Pakistani ambassador to the United States at the time, Husain Haqqani, had colluded with Pakistani American businessman Mansoor Ijaz to draft a memo to then Joint Chiefs of Staff chairman Mike Mullen. The memo offered to reform the ISI by eliminating its Section S charged with maintaining ties with militants, in exchange for US support to prevent a purported military coup.[18]

The unsigned memo, according to businessman Ijaz, had been drafted on the orders of President Zardari in the wake of the US raid on bin Laden, which had demoralized the army and embarrassed Zardari's weakened government. Ambassador Haqqani denied having written the memo, and the Zardari government backed him up. Pressured by the army, a Pakistani Supreme Court three-member commission was set up to investigate the matter. In June 2012, the commission concluded that Ambassador Haqqani was behind the controversial memo and found that he was "not loyal" to the Pakistani state, having sought to undermine the country's nuclear assets, armed forces, and intelligence agency.[19] The ambassador, who had resigned and returned to his previous position as a professor at Boston University, responded that the Supreme Court was politically motivated and had abused its authority.

In the meantime, allegations from diplomatic cables made public by WikiLeaks resurfaced, citing Vice President Joe Biden and then US ambassador to Islamabad Anne Patterson, announcing that Zardari felt that the head of the ISI and General Kayani could remove him from office at any time and that Kayani himself, in a conversation with Patterson, had admitted that he "might, however reluctantly," pressure President Zardari to resign and presumably leave Pakistan.[20] The coup rumors led Prime Minister Gilani to publicly denounce "conspiracies that are being hatched to pack up the elected government," and, stopping short of accusing the armed forces of plotting a takeover, warned that the military "cannot be a state within a state."[21] The following day, army chief General Kayani responded that the "army will continue to support the democratic process in the country" and labeled talks of a coup as "a bogey to divert the focus from the real issues."[22]

To end an already bad year for US-Pakistani ties, on November 26, NATO aircraft killed twenty-four Pakistani soldiers in strikes against two military posts in Salala, on the northwestern border with Afghanistan, in what Pakistan portrayed as "unprovoked acts of blatant aggression." The government in Islamabad reacted by ordering the CIA to remove the drone operations at Shamsi Air Base and, more importantly, closing down the two main NATO supply routes into Afghanistan.[23] In Washington, suggestions for President Obama to offer a formal apology were turned down, as, particularly during an election year in the United States, the condolences given were deemed sufficient until the incident was fully investigated.

This pattern of mutual distrust, blame, and anger has undermined the bilateral relationship, and getting back to normal has demanded ever greater efforts. But the two countries need each other.

The United States needs Pakistan to facilitate peace talks with the Taliban as part of the American exit strategy from Afghanistan. Thus, in the midst of the bilateral confrontation over the Haqqani attack on the US embassy in Kabul, the Obama administration was relying on the same Pakistani intelligence services that support the Haqqani network to help start reconciliation talks aimed at ending the war in Afghanistan. In January 2012, Taliban negotiators declared that they had begun meeting with US officials in Qatar, with the support of the Pakistani government. Secretary of State Hillary Clinton characterized the new approach as "fight, talk, build," combining the push for reconciliation with the continuation of drone attacks.[24]

Pakistan will mind its own interests in the reconciliation talks, promoting separate agreements with the Afghan government so as to advance its own interests in Afghanistan after American forces withdraw. For Islamabad, there cannot be a peace deal with the Taliban without their explicit support.

Following the Salala air strikes, the newly formed Defense of Pakistan Council (DPC), gathering about forty Islamist groups, began to organize rallies opposing the reopening of the NATO supply lines and decrying Pakistan's strengthening of ties with the United States and India. Interestingly, the DPC's chief coordinator is Hamid Gul, the former ISI chief identified by Benazir Bhutto as a suspect in case she were to be assassinated, a fact that raised suspicions about the involvement of the intelligence establishment in this new radical group.[25]

The US defense secretary Leon Panetta, speaking in New Delhi in June 2012 at a conference on Indo-US defense relations, warned that Washington was reaching "the limits of our patience" with Pakistan regarding safe havens that allow "terrorists to use their country as a safety net in order to conduct their attacks on our forces."[26] At about the same time, the CIA announced that a drone strike in Pakistan's tribal belt had killed Al-Qaida's deputy leader, Abu Yahya al-Libi.

The Salala impasse was resolved by another demonstration of reluctant pragmatism by both sides: On July 3, 2012, Secretary of State Clinton presented a carefully worded declaration—which avoided the word *apology*—regretting the incidents of November

2011 that left twenty-four Pakistani troops dead, offering condolences to the families of the soldiers and expressing, along with her Pakistani colleague Foreign Minister Hina Rabbani Khar, that "we are sorry for losses suffered by both our countries in this fight against terrorism." At the same time, the two countries announced the reopening of the ground supply routes into Afghanistan without levying any additional transit fees.[27]

PAKISTAN'S STRATEGIC POSTURE views the militant groups that the United States wants destroyed as proxies in the bitter rivalry with its larger and more powerful neighbor, India. While Washington seeks to defeat Al-Qaida and its Islamic militant associates, Pakistani leaders take a longer view toward their own interests, which means accepting tactical cooperation with the United States without losing sight of the goal of gaining strategic depth in Afghanistan and defending their country against India.

Pakistan has noted with great concern the expansion of India's presence in Afghanistan, particularly after the May 2011 visit by Prime Minister Manmohan Singh when he promised to increase India's aid to Kabul from $1.5 to $2 billion. President Hamid Karzai's following visit to New Delhi in September 2011 unsettled Islamabad further, especially when it was announced that the two countries had reached an agreement for India to train Afghan army officers after NATO left Afghanistan. Reportedly, the Pakistanis were angry at the United States for not having impeded this training accord.[28]

The US tilt toward India, reflected in President Barack Obama's November 2010 visit to New Delhi, and not Islamabad, disappointed Pakistan, as did Obama's endorsement of India's bid for permanent membership on the UN Security Council. Pakistan had already considered the Indo-US civil nuclear agreement of 2005 to have fundamentally altered the strategic balance in South Asia, and the relaxation of US export restrictions on Indian space agencies, following Obama's visit to New Delhi, only confirmed the status quo.

Considering Indian superiority in conventional forces, Pakistan has invested more heavily in nuclear weapons. The country has more nuclear weapons than India—having overtaken Great Britain as the world's fifth-largest nuclear weapons power—and its inventories of weapons-usable fissile materials are larger than those of New Delhi.[29] The nuclear rivalry was once more noted in Pakistan's successful test launch of an improved intermediate-range ballistic missile capable of carrying a nuclear warhead, six days after India test fired its Agni-V intercontinental ballistic missile, which has a range of over five thousand kilometers, making it capable of reaching Beijing and Shanghai.

Pakistan sees a better ally in China than in the United States. After the bin Laden raid, Pakistan turned to China to regain leverage with the United States. During a four-day visit to Beijing, Prime Minister Yousuf Raza Gilani concluded a coproduction agreement to immediately provide Pakistan with fifty JF-17 Thunder fighter jets, which would be followed by more fighter aircraft with stealth technology. As part of that high-level visit, Defense Minister Chaudhry Ahmed Mukhtar announced that Islamabad had asked the Chinese to "please build a naval base at Gwadar," a deepwater port in the Arabian Sea, west of Karachi, the construction of which China had invested heavily in.[30] China and Pakistan do share strategic interests regarding India, and Beijing also needs Islamabad as a check on ties between Islamist separatists from the Xinjiang region and Pakistani jihadists. However, China could hardly offset Pakistan's relationship with the United States.

Pakistan would certainly like to reduce what many regard as

an overdependence on the United States. For Pakistan, the history of bilateral ties is one of betrayal by Washington dating back to the 1960s when, after remaining close friends with Pakistan for a decade, the United States stayed neutral when Pakistan went to war with India in 1965. Pakistanis remember well that the United States used the jihadists against the Soviet Union in Afghanistan, and as President Zardari wrote in a *Washington Post* op-ed piece, "once the Soviets were defeated, the Americans took the next bus out of town, leaving behind a political vacuum that ultimately led to the Talibanization of Afghanistan, the birth of Al Qaida and the current jihadist insurrection in Pakistan."[31]

These same themes emerged in a conversation I had in 2010 with a high Pakistani official during a dinner in Islamabad, when he asked me what had happened to Chilean dictator Augusto Pinochet. After I told my interlocutor that the dictator had died in 2006, he said, "Here in Pakistan we have our own Pinochets created by the United States who are killing our people, like Mullah Omar, Hakimullah Mehsud, and Baitullah."

"Well, Pinochet ended up becoming a problem for the Americans," I interjected.

"The Americans always seek short-term gains and end up reaping long-term hate and crisis," he responded.

I asked how he viewed the Barack Obama administration.

"If we don't move against the Taliban, we could forgo democracy and the army will rule directly. I don't think President Obama will ignore the dangers to our rule of law. He doesn't have a choice. He has to mind Pakistan, because terrorism and nuclear arms are the new Cold War."

MUTUAL DISTRUST BETWEEN the United States and Pakistan will likely continue, although improvements can occur. So long as Pakistan pursues its national interests—and it is perfectly legitimate that it would do so—its intelligence agencies will pragmatically preserve ties with Islamist extremists, just as once the United States found it expedient to ally with people like bin Laden and other jihadists against the Soviet Union. Pakistan's prudence is justified when it is asked by the United States to kill Pakistani Taliban militants and, at the same time, use its influence to bring them to the bargaining table.

It would not be surprising that both the United States and Pakistan will continue their respective "double-dealings." Pakistan won't stop giving sanctuary to the Taliban and dealing with militants, but at the same time, it cannot afford to abandon its alliance with Washington and the sizable aid it brings.[32] Washington, in turn, will prod Islamabad to go after the extremists that kill US troops and will attack the Taliban and Al-Qaida with drones or SEAL teams if necessary, notwithstanding Pakistani government opposition. The United States will likely preserve normal intelligence ties with the ISI to limit the danger of further instability and to pursue its goal of keeping Pakistani nuclear weapons from falling into Taliban or Al-Qaida hands.

WikiLeaks' cache of US State Department cables released in late 2010 showed the mutual complicity between Washington and Islamabad on sensitive issues like the drone attacks. One such cable revealed that then prime minister Gilani gave approval to the US drone campaign in Pakistan's tribal area, suggesting that Islamabad would protest publicly but then ignore the problem.[33] A *New York Times* investigation found that secret negotiations had yielded a deal as far back as 2004 by which the CIA would kill enemies of Pakistan's army with drone attacks, and the ISI would allow regular CIA drone flights over the tribal areas to strike at US enemies. Washington would never acknowledge targeted missile killings and Islamabad would either assume credit or remain silent on the specific hits.[34] Musharraf did not think it would be too difficult to hide the deal: "In Pakistan, things fall out of the sky all the time,"[35] he allegedly told a CIA officer. But by 2013, drone attacks had become highly controversial, mobilizing opposition Pakistani politician and former cricket star Imran Khan and American activists in peace marches in the tribal regions to demand an end to drone strikes, and generating criticism from former US ambassador to Pakistan Cameron Munter about their excessive use. In the United States, public debate and criticism mounted regarding the drone strikes policy, while a United Nations special rapporteur on human rights and counterterrorism commented that the use of U.S drones is a "violation of Pakistan's sovereignty" and breaks down "tribal structures."[36]

There have been unintended consequences of the bilateral double games. Pakistan used to be a country of sophisticated and secular elites admired by the West, but now it is growingly polarized between those who envision a modern, pluralist society and those who adhere to the intolerant and conservative version of Islamism. More and more Pakistanis have become anti-American and detractors of the West. In 2012 a survey by the Pew Research Center showed that anti-American sentiment runs deep in Pakistan: 74 percent of respondents considered the United States an enemy—up from 69 percent in 2011 and 64 percent in 2008.[37] The bilateral climate witnessed an improvement with Senator John Kerry as the US secretary of state of the second Obama administration, as Kerry has been behind the normalization of previously held-up Pentagon reimbursements to Pakistan for the stationing of troops on the border with Afghanistan, has frequently served as an unofficial envoy to Pakistan, and is considered by Islamabad to be sympathetic to its concerns.

Pakistanis are increasingly divided between urban and rural, the educated and the illiterate, and by competing religious identities that erode the common idea of their nation. Most Pakistanis reject terrorism and Islamic extremism, but assigning the blame for the deaths of 4,447 persons in 476 major terrorist attacks in 2011 becomes blurred as jihadist ideology has penetrated Pakistani society. There are many who fault the arrogance of American power or fault the lack of economic and social progress derived from Washington's millions. In the meantime, Pakistan is less secure than it was a decade ago, and many believe that it—not Afghanistan—has become the main battleground of the confrontation between the global jihad and counterterrorism.

Benazir Bhutto would have probably had difficulties in selling reconciliation and a pluralist society in such a context. Two senior politicians, Punjab governor Salman Taseer and Minorities Minister Shahbaz Bhatti, were assassinated in 2011 as they called for amendments to the controversial blasphemy law.[38] Governor Taseer was assassinated by his Elite Force bodyguard who declared he had murdered the governor because Taseer had criticized the blasphemy law in a case involving an accused Christian woman.

A controversy in September 2012 involving the arrest of a Christian girl in a slum on the outskirts of Islamabad, accused by an Islamic cleric of supposedly burning pages of a religious text used to teach the Koran to children, caused Christian residents to flee from a community that, until then, had lived peacefully beside a Muslim majority. The case experienced an about-face when the Muslim cleric was arrested for planting evidence to incriminate the girl, who was subsequently released and the charges against her were dropped. Shortly thereafter, the shooting of schoolgirl Malala Yousafzai by Taliban gunmen for advocating access to education for girls in her Swat Valley residence generated a wave of protests and outrage in Pakistan and throughout the world. In 2013 Malala recuperated from her head wounds after surgery in Britain, she gave a moving speech about girls' education and women's empowerment at the UN General Assembly, and a fund set up in her name to benefit girls' education in Pakistan and Afghanistan had gathered significant resources. In the meantime, the Taliban has extended its reach of power and influence well beyond the country's frontier region, as demonstrated in its reported growing presence in large cities such as Karachi.[39]

Domestic political instability has been aggravated by the growing confrontation between Pakistan's Supreme Court and the elected civilian government of President Zardari. The Supreme Court has engaged in judicial activism dictating the price of sugar and fuel, directing the traffic in Karachi, and, more significantly, reviving a thirteen-year-old inquiry into accusations of election rigging by the ISI that aimed at ousting Benazir Bhutto in favor of Nawaz Sharif.

The Supreme Court forced out Prime Minister Yousuf Raza Gilani for refusing its order to send a written request to Swiss authorities asking that they reopen a corruption probe against Zardari dating back to the 1990s. The court continued its assault on the Zardari government by blocking the nomination of Makhdoom Shahabuddin, hours after he had been chosen as the nominee to replace Gilani as prime minister. President Zardari then nominated Raja Pervez Ashraf, a former minister of water and power, as prime minister, winning the approval of Parliament. The Supreme Court reissued the new prime minister the order to write a letter to the Swiss authorities requesting that they reopen the graft case against Zardari, which he eventually did in a draft approved consensually by the court and the government.

The escalating confrontations between the judiciary and the civilian authorities have exacerbated concerns about the fate of

Pakistani democracy. Many have sided with the judges in their campaign against corruption and in favor of the rule of law. But critics argue that the Supreme Court acts only rapidly and effectively against the government, that it is slow when cases affect the opposition or accused terrorists, and that it is all rhetoric and little action when it comes to situations impacting the military.[40]

COULD BENAZIR BHUTTO have changed this state of affairs? Very likely she would have sought to diminish tensions with India,[41] rein in the ISI, protect the rights of secular minorities, and advocate peace talks with the Taliban much earlier than what is now recognized as necessary. Perhaps she would have moved gradually to strengthen civilian institutions, reducing the army's role in politics.

In her two stints as prime minister, Benazir exhibited major political faults. She was politically naive at times, arrogant, and power hungry; she compromised rule-of-law principles and values, cared more about the form rather than the substance of governing, and was undoubtedly involved in corruption scandals. Such a disappointing track record made some observers skeptical about what she could have accomplished for her country. But in recent times, she had evolved, according to abundant witnesses. She had become more humble, politically mature, and willing to do the hard work involved in the democratic reconstruction of her country.

Benazir Bhutto might have placed a strong focus on a key issue for Pakistan's present and future: socioeconomic development. Knowing the United States as few politicians do, she would have lobbied not only for economic and military aid but also for easing trade barriers for Pakistani goods and services, thus creating jobs and a larger middle class, and incorporating more women into the job market. Creating conditions for the return or reengagement of many highly trained Pakistani professionals who live abroad would have been her concern.

Trade, not just aid, seems to be key for a more economically independent and prosperous Pakistan. But worsening security conditions in the country have driven some industries, like textiles, to move operations to Bangladesh, where wages are lower and exports enjoy preferential access to the European Union market, unlike what occurs with goods originating in Pakistan.

These days, Pakistan faces an economic meltdown, with crippling inflation, high unemployment, and an energy crisis that results in power outages that can last up to sixteen hours at a time.[42] Only about half of the population has access to electricity, but even this segment experiences frequent blackouts and shortages. Pakistan's growing urbanization and industrialization demand more energy, but the production capacity of energy remains weak and its distribution system outmoded. Despite the fact that the country has considerable energy resources, including gas, nuclear, coal, wind, and hydropower, and that it exported electricity to India in the past, it depends heavily on energy imports and is projected to undergo a sevenfold increase in its energy demand by 2030.[43]

Although progress has been made in increasing net primary school enrollment rates and even though literacy rates are rising fast, at least among men, schooling disparities are severe, ranging from 2.4 years of schooling for the poorest income quintile to 8.9 years for the richest. Its under-5 mortality rate is one of the highest in Asia and malnutrition remains at critical levels. Agricultural production has been dropping steadily over the years, and the country is now importing wheat, as rural poverty has increased. Remittances from the millions of Pakistanis living and working abroad have alleviated a situation of economic hardship that is causing rising levels of frustration and tension.

Pakistan is a rich country, but 33 percent of its people live below the poverty line,[44] while the tax-to-GDP ratio is a low 10 percent, compared to the 15 percent average for developing nations. Tax avoidance, more than tax evasion, is a major additional problem, as fewer than one million Pakistanis voluntarily file income tax, a rate that is among the lowest in the world. Out of the 39.1 million people employed, only 2.14 million pay taxes, and almost none of these taxes are generated in the high-income bracket, thus requiring the extension of the narrow taxation base that affects the elite.[45] In an interview with the *Financial Times*, Pakistan's wealthiest person, Mian Muhammad Mansha, admitted that people like him "should pay more taxes."[46] A 2013 report of the international development select committee of the UK House of Commons stated that "any increase in the UK's official development assistance to Pakistan must be conditional on Pakistan increasing its tax collection and widening the tax base."[47] The report further pointed out that seventy percent of the members of the Pakistani parliament do not file a tax return.

Benazir Bhutto wanted development change in her country, a more balanced equation in the ties between the civilian and military elite, and a strengthening of the political institutions of democracy. She wanted to overcome the Cold War mentality that assigned too many resources to security for a hypothetical confrontation with Pakistan's rising Indian neighbor. She would have probably appealed to the United States to seek some regional understanding to bring Pakistan, India, and China together on nuclear matters, to make some significant headway with India regarding the Kashmir issue, and to stabilize Pakistan's poorly demarcated border with Afghanistan.

Bhutto would have probably made a good case in Washington that the main challenge in the region is Pakistan, not

Afghanistan, and that such a recognition would require stabilization and socioeconomic development, as much as shared responsibilities to confront the extremist threat. Equally important, she might have urged the implementation of reforms in taxation, land distribution, education, and rule of law, alongside the provision of massive investments in infrastructure, water, energy, agriculture, trade, job creation, and combating poverty and inequality. She would have probably convinced the United States that such a hefty challenge would require time, patience, and sustained support. Benazir Bhutto wanted to prove wrong those who asserted that Pakistan was condemned to remain a "failed state." She aspired to make sustainable democracy a reality.

When Nawaz Sharif was inaugurated as the country's new prime minister in June 2013, following his PML-N party victory in the parliamentary elections held in May of that year, Pakistan witnessed for the first time a civilian elected government—that of the PPP—completing its five-year term and handing over power to another democratically elected government. In another first, the election process was organized and overseen by a democratically designated caretaker government that ceased its functions when Sharif assumed office. Further, Mamnoon Hussain, a close ally of prime minister Nawaz Sharif, was subsequently elected president of Pakistan by legislators of both houses of the national parliament and four provincial assemblies, replacing Asif Ali Zardari.

The Taliban threats of violence and the attacks during the campaign that left more than one hundred people dead did not deter voters. Turnout in the May 2013 elections was about 60 percent, a hefty increase from the 44 percent registered in 2008. First-time voters comprised 34 percent of all registered voters. European Union election observers stated that at 90 percent of the polling stations monitored, the conduct of the election was satisfactory or good. The electoral rolls had been cleaned of "ghost voters" that in the past had enabled vote rigging. This is what Benazir wished to see in her country. Her assassination may have marked a turning point toward a far-reaching demand for tangible strides in democratic governance and the repudiation of violence, terrorism, and development stagnation.

Sharif, at times a political rival but also an ally of Bhutto in the recuperation of democracy, was elected with a strong mandate to mend his country's broken economy and to confront other daunting domestic and external challenges, including a new relationship with the United States. Benazir paved the way with her political message that advocated the promotion of an economically and politically stable and enlarging middle class, which she saw as fundamental to sustain democracy in Pakistan. In her posthumously published book, *Reconciliation*, she proposed a "Marshall Plan" to improve the lives of people in Pakistan and other Muslim nations, arguing that if the West pursued the road of development, it would reap moral and pragmatic gains, just as the US image improved in opinion polls following the sizable American relief to the victims of Pakistan's 2005 earthquake that killed almost ninety thousand people. "Economic reconstruction can help turn the Muslim street around,"[48] argued Benazir Bhutto, and this is probably the surest way to achieve the dreams she had for Pakistan that vanished on that fateful evening of December 27, 2007, at Liaquat Bagh in Rawalpindi.

Acknowledgments

THIS BOOK TOOK more than two years to write. It began as a work intended to reveal the behind-the-scenes story of the United Nations commission inquiry into the assassination of Benazir Bhutto, and it turned into a larger story about the Bhutto clan, Pakistani politics, US-Pakistani ties, and the threats to democracy posed by extremism and thwarted development.

I owe a debt of gratitude to several people who helped me in the task of conceiving and then writing this book, while learning a great deal in the process.

My literary agent Fredrica Friedman encouraged me to envisage a more ambitious book than I had planned, and wisely guided me in the process of preparing a sound proposal. I am immensely thankful to Tom Mayer, senior editor at W. W. Norton & Company, who gave me substantive advice, polished my first draft, animated me to dig deeper into many issues, and was personally supportive of my research and writing throughout the process. Ryan Harrington, Tom's assistant at W. W. Norton, attended patiently and efficiently to the many details of the book's production. Kristin Roth ably edited my manuscript, polishing language and drafting style.

My friend and UN colleague Helen Clark, former prime minister of New Zealand and administrator of the United Nations Development Programme, read the entire initial draft, encouraged me to complete the project, and provided me with valuable substantive and editorial suggestions. I am also very appreciative to writer Ahmed Rashid, a noted authority on Pakistani affairs, and to my commission colleague Peter Fitzgerald, both of whom read the manuscript of the book and gave me praiseful comments and concrete ideas. Richard Haass, president of the Council on Foreign Relations, also read the manuscript and afforded me a thoughtful reflection and collegial encouragement.

I am particularly thankful to Ambassador Zalmay Khalilzad, former US envoy to Afghanistan and esteemed colleague from the period we coincided at the United Nations as ambassadors of our respective countries. Zal and his wife, Dr. Cheryl Benard, knew Benazir Bhutto, and they granted me valuable information about her views and state of mind before she returned to Pakistan in 2007; they also read the full manuscript, providing me with detailed comments on both substance and style.

Last but not least, my wife Pamela, always my supporter and source of inspiration, backed me throughout the research and writing process that used up many weekends and vacations and, at times, helped me with research and drafting queries. My daughter Paloma, an academic in her own right, regularly demanded updates on my writing progress that stimulated me to push ahead.

Finally, I thank the people of Pakistan, whom I learned to appreciate and admire during the interactions I had with them in Pakistan and abroad. Their country deserves the best.

HERALDO MUÑOZ
New York, June 2013

Notes

Preface

1 Ali Sethi, "Lahore Murder Mystery," *New York Times*, March 4, 2009.

2 See "Letter dated 2 February 2009 from the Secretary-General to the President of the Security Council," UN Security Council, S/2009/67, February 3, 2009.

3 "Letter dated 3 February 2009 from the President of the Security Council to the Secretary-General," UN Security Council, S/2009 /68, February 3, 2009.

4 See Bill Varner, "Bhutto's Death to Be Probed for UN by Chile's Munoz, Envoy Says," Bloomberg.com, February 3, 2009.

5 Benazir Bhutto quoted by Ian Jack, "Benazir Bhutto," *Vanity Fair*, May 1986, www.vanityfair.com/culture/features/1986/05/Bhutto -198605.

6 William Dalrymple, "Pakistan's flawed and feudal princess," *Guardian*, Saturday, December 29, 2007.

7 See, for example, "Victim of the System," *Hindu*, April 23, 2010.

1: A Murder Foretold

1 See "A Conversation with Benazir Bhutto," transcript, Council on Foreign Relations, New York, August 15, 2007, 2–3.

2 Ibid., 5.

3 Ibid., 7.

4 Ibid., 4.

5 Benazir Bhutto, "When I Return to Pakistan," *Washington Post*, September 20, 2007.

6 Benazir Bhutto, according to episode narrated to the author by Cheryl Benard, May 2013.

7 See Benazir Bhutto, *Reconciliation: Islam, Democracy and the West* (New York: Harper Perennial, 2008), 219–220.

8 See "After bombing, Bhutto assails officials' ties," *New York Times*, October 20, 2007.

9 See Haroon Siddique, "Detective Withdraws from Bhutto Attack Investigation," *Guardian*, October 24, 2007.

10 Musharraf quoted by "Musharraf, Benazir vow to fight extremism," Zeenews.com, October 20, 2007, http://zeenews.india.com/print.aspx?nid=402390.

11 The word *bagh* means "garden" and is used typically in South and Southeast Asian countries. The word *bagh* is common to Persian, Urdu, and other languages and refers to an enclosed area with trees, shrubs, flowers, and other vegetation.

12 Laura King, "In Pakistan, It Was a Rally Like Many Others," *Los Angeles Times*, December 28, 2007.

13 Salman Masood and Carlotta Gall, "Bhutto Assassination Ignites Disarray," *New York Times*, December 28, 2007.

14 See M. Ylyas Khan, "Bhutto murder: Key questions," BBC News, February 8, 2008.

15 See "Benazir Bhutto killed in attack," BBC News, December 27, 2007.

16 Farooq Naek quoted by "Benazir aide says government explanation 'pack of lies'" *Dawn,* December 29, 2007. http://archives.dawn.com/2007/12/29/top6.htm.

17 Bahzad Alam Khan, "Telltale Images Expose Fatal Security Flaws: Benazir's Assassination," *Dawn*, December 30, 2007.

18 Masood and Gall, "Bhutto Assassination Ignites Disarray."

19 Isambard Wilkinson, Richard Edwards, and David Blair, "Pakistan Faces Horror of Civil War after Benazir Bhutto Is Assassinated in Suicide Attack," *Telegraph*, December 27, 2007.

20 "Bhutto Attacker Identified, Servant under Scanner," RTT News, January 9, 2008.

21 See Joby Warrick, "CIA Places Blame for Bhutto Assassination," *Washington Post,* January 18, 2008, A1.

22 Ibid.

23 Senator Safdar Abbasi quoted by Bruce Loudon, "Who Killed Benazir?," *Australian Magazine*, September 19, 2009.

24 Naheed Khan quoted by ibid.

25 Asif Ali Zardari, "The Duty My Wife Left Us," *Washington Post,* January 5, 2008.

2: An Early History of Instability

1 Syed Muhammad Zulqurnain Zaidi, "The Assassination of the Prime Minister Liaquat Ali Khan: The Fateful Journey," *Pakistan Journal of History and Culture* 31, no. 1 (2010): 71.

2 See Owen Bennet-Jones, "Questions Concerning the Murder of Benazir Bhutto," *London Review of Books* 34, no. 23 (December 6, 2012): 10.

3 See Shahid Saeed, "Murder at Company Bagh," *Friday Times*, Pakistan, March 25, 2011, 26.

4 Zaidi, "The Assassination of the Prime Minister Liaquat Ali Khan," 85.

5 On Jinnah's political life and legacy, see Stanley Wolpert, *Jinnah of Pakistan* (New York: Oxford University Press, 1999).

6 See Jamsheed Marker, *Quiet Diplomacy: Memoirs of an Ambassador of Pakistan* (Oxford: Oxford University Press, 2010), 116.

3: Violence in the Family and in the Nation

1 See Benazir Bhutto, *Daughter of Destiny: An Autobiography* (New York: Harper Perennial, 2008), 48.

2 Ibid., 70.

3 Zia ul-Haq quoted by William Richter, "The Political Dynamics of Islamic Resurgence in Pakistan," *Asian Survey* 19, no. 6 (June 1979): 555.

4 The poisoned mangoes theory inspired the novel by Mohammed Hanif, *A Case of Exploding Mangoes* (London: Jonathan Cape, 2008).

5 See James Bone and Zahid Hussain, "As Pakistan Comes Full Circle, a Light Is Shone on Zia ul-Haq's Death," *Times*, London, August 16, 2008.

6 Hamid Gul quoted by ibid.

7 See Barbara Crossette, "Who Killed Zia," *World Policy Journal* (Fall 2005): 96. Crossette thoroughly analyzed the case, including details from a lengthy interview with former ambassador Dean, whose career was cut short due to the Israeli involvement theory, which he advocated internally in the State Department.

8 Vernon A. Walters, *The Mighty and the Meek: Dispatches from the Front Line of Diplomacy* (London: Little, Brown Book Limited, 2001), 197.

9 Crossette, "Who Killed Zia," 95.

10 See Jane Perlez and Victoria Burnett, "Benazir Bhutto, 54, Lived in the Eye of Pakistan Storm," *New York Times*, December 28, 2007.

11 Benazir Bhutto, *Daughter of Destiny*, 357.

12 Ibid., 285.

13 According to Fatima Bhutto, Benazir opposed blaming the CIA and the ISI for Shah's murder. Benazir supposedly was bent on cooperating with Washington and avoiding confrontation with the

West. See Fatima Bhutto, *Songs of Blood and Sword: A Daughter's Memoir* (New York: Nation Books, 2010), 257–260.

14 Benazir Bhutto, *Daughter of Destiny*, 405.

15 Benazir Bhutto quoted by Rory McCarthy, "'I never asked for power,'" *Guardian,* Wednesday, August 14, 2002.

16 Benazir Bhutto quoted by Hassan Abbas, *Pakistan's Drift into Extremism: Allah, the Army, and America's War on Terror* (Armonk, New York: M.E. Sharpe, 2005), 142.

17 Benazir Bhutto, *Daughter of Destiny*, 412.

18 Ibid., 282–283.

19 See Fatima Bhutto, *Songs of Blood and Sword*, 208.

20 Ibid., 312.

21 Benazir offered her brother parole and house arrest during the Eid holiday, but Mir Murtaza refused, demanding the same parole for all political prisoners.

22 Raja Anwar, *The Terrorist Prince: The Life and Death of Murtaza Bhutto* (London: Verso, 1997), 200.

23 See Tariq Ali, "Daughter of the West," *London Review of Books* 29, no. 24 (December 13, 2007): 13.

24 Anwar, *The Terrorist Prince*, 208.

25 Fatima Bhutto, *Songs of Blood and Sword*, 402–403.

26 Benazir Bhutto, *Daughter of Destiny*, 421.

27 Opposition leader Nawaz Sharif accused the Benazir Bhutto government of state terrorism against its political opponents. See "Benazir Bhutto Accused in Brother's Death," CNN World, September 21, 1996, http://www.cnn.com/WORLD/9609/21/pakistan.bhutto/.

28 See John F. Burns, "House of Graft: Tracing the Bhutto Millions—a Special Report," *New York Times*, January 9, 1998.

29 Rory McCarthy, "'I never asked for power.'"

30 See Peter R. Blood, "Pakistan-U.S. Relations," Congressional Research Service, The Library of Congress, March 10, 2002, 6.

The Supreme Court judges found many indications that the trial against Bhutto had been rigged.

31 Pervez Musharraf, *In the Line of Fire: A Memoir* (New York: Free Press, 2006), 106.

32 Benazir Bhutto quoted by Ahmed Rashid, *Descent into Chaos: The US and the Disaster in Pakistan, Afghanistan, and Central Asia* (London: Penguin Books, 2008), 52.

33 Musharraf quoted by Ikram Sehgal, "The president who never was," *Defence Journal*, July 2001. http://www.defencejournal.com/2001/july/president.htm.

4: On the Road to Islamabad

1 "Benazir Murder: UN Probe Team in Pakistan," *Hindu*, February 2, 2010. http://www.thehindu.com/news/international/benazir-murder-un-probe-team-in-pakistan/article99249.ece.

2 Declan Walsh, "UN Team Arrives in Pakistan for Inquiry into Benazir Bhutto's Death," *Guardian*, July 16, 2009.

3 Ali, "Daughter of the West," 3.

4 Maqsood Tirmizi, "UN Not to Name Culprits in BB Murder Case," *Nation*, Pakistan, July 18, 2009, 8.

5 Ayman al-Zawahiri quoted by Scott Stewart, "Pakistan: Biting the Hand that Feeds You," Stratfor.com weekly, October 7, 2009, 4. http://www.stratfor.com/weekly/20091007_pakistan_biting_hand_feeds_you.

6 See "Bhutto Assassination: UN Wants to Quiz Musharraf," Allvoices.com, November 6, 2009. http://www.allvoices.com/news/4562167-quiz-musharraf/s/41555399-benazir-murder-case.

5: The US Gravitas in Pakistani Affairs

1 See Musharraf, *In the Line of Fire*, 201.

2 Dialogue quoted by Zahid Hussain, "A General turn around," *Newsline*, February 14, 2003. http://www.newslinemagazine.com/2003/02/a-general-turn-around/.

3 Chamberlin quoted by Musharraf, *In the Line of Fire*, 205.

4 Muhammad Ali Jinnah quoted by Dennis Kux, *Disenchanted Allies: The United States and Pakistan, 1947–2000* (Baltimore and London: Johns Hopkins University Press, 2001), 20.

5 Liaquat Ali Khan quoted by ibid., 3.

6 Ayub Khan quoted by ibid., 57.

7 Richard Nixon quoted by ibid., 61.

8 Mohammed Ayub Khan, *Friends Not Masters* (London: Oxford University Press) cited in ibid., 74.

9 Lyndon Johnson quoted by ibid., 148.

10 Dennis Kux, *Disenchanted Allies*, 177.

11 See Margaret Macmillan, *Nixon and Mao: The Week that Changed the World* (New York: Random House, 2007), 221.

12 Ibid., 224.

13 Abdul Qadeer Khan, a metallurgist by profession, had been working in a uranium-enrichment facility in the Netherlands when he offered his services to the government of Pakistan, becoming the father of the country's nuclear weapons program. When the US government presented evidence to Musharraf in September 2003 that A. Q. Khan was involved in nuclear proliferation activities, the government put him under house arrest.

14 Adrian Levy and Catherine Scott-Clark, *Deception: Pakistan, the United States, and the Secret Trade in Nuclear Weapons* (New York: Walker & Company, 2007), 48.

15 See Marker, *Quiet Diplomacy*, 274.

16 Ibid., 298.

17 Abdul Salam Zaeef, *My Life with the Taliban* (New York: Columbia University Press, 2010), 33.

18 Rashid, *Descent into Chaos*, 10.

19 "Punish Pakistan's Perfidy on the Bomb," *New York Times*, July 17, 1987.

20 Bhutto quoted by Kux, *Disenchanted Allies*, 302.

21 See Hassan Abbas, *Pakistan's Drift into Extremism*, 140.

22 Marker, *Quiet Diplomacy*, 339.

23 See the detailed discussion on the subject in ibid., 340–41.

24 Bill Clinton, *My Life* (New York: Alfred A. Knopf, 2004), 864–65.

25 Ibid., 865.

26 See Abbas, *Pakistan's Drift into Extremism*, 176.

27 US ambassador William Milam quoted by Rashid, *Descent into Chaos*, 48.

28 Ibid., 50.

29 See ibid., 4.

30 Ibid., 3. Pakistan's influence with the Taliban in Kabul was such that Karzai said that once he was called by the Pakistani Foreign Office to discuss the modalities of him becoming the Taliban's envoy to the UN. (See ibid., 13–14.)

31 Richard Armitage, quoted by ibid., 58.

32 Ibid., 78.

33 See Seymour Hersh, "The Getaway," *New York Times*, November 24, 2001.

34 George W. Bush quoted by Joshua Kurlantzick, "Musharraf for Brains," *New Republic*, March 26, 2008.

35 George W. Bush, Public Papers of the President of the United States, 2002, Book 1, US Government Printing Office, February 13, 2002, 1.

36 Teresita C. Schaffer, "U.S. Influence on Pakistan: Can Partners Have Divergent Priorities?" *Washington Quarterly* (Winter 2002–03): 179.

37 See Mariane Pearl, *A Mighty Heart* (New York: Scribner, 2003), 182.

38 Mushahid Hussain, "Pakistan's Washington Embrace Loosens," *Asia Times*, September 14, 2002. http://www.atimes.com/atimes/printN.html.

39 Condoleezza Rice quoted by ibid.

40 US intelligence did not detect these activities until late 2005 because surveillance satellite capability, covert command strength and other assets along the Afghan-Pakistani border did not exist, as these resources had been shifted to the Iraq war surge. See Heraldo Muñoz, *A Solitary War: A Diplomat's Chronicle of the Iraq War and Its Lessons* (Golden, Colorado: Fulcrum, 2008), 20-21.

41 Rashid, *Descent into Chaos*, 229.

42 Musharraf, *In the Line of Fire*, 250.

43 In 2005 the White House had subscribed to an agreement with India to sell it nuclear fuel and reactors for its civilian nuclear program, while denying a similar deal with Pakistan.

44 See Madeleine K. Albright quoted in "Pakistan Is World's 'Most Dangerous Country' Ex-US Official Says," *Global Security Newswire*, February 2, 2009.

45 Condoleezza Rice, *No Higher Honor: A Memoir of My Years in Washington* (New York: Crown Publishers, 2011), 608.

6: The US-Brokered Return of Bhutto to Her Homeland

1 See Adrian Levy and Cathy Scott-Clark, "The Plot to Bring Back Benazir," *Guardian*, July 20, 2007. See also "The Story behind 'Benazir-Musharraf Contacts,'" *Dawn*, Pakistan, July 22, 2007.

2 See Benazir Bhutto, *Reconciliation: Islam, Democracy and the West* (New York: Harper Perennial, 2008), 227–228.

3 See "The Story behind 'Benazir-Musharraf Contacts.'"

4 See Benazir Bhutto interview with Dean Nelson, "Defiant Bhutto plans return," *Sunday Times*, April 15, 2007.

5 Rice, *No Higher Honor*, 609.

6 Ibid., 210.

7 See "2007: Patterson Urges Tariq Aziz to Provide for Benazir's Security," *Dawn*, May 22, 2011.

8 See Ron Suskind, *The Way of the World: A Story of Truth and Hope in an Age of Extremism* (New York: Harper Perennial, 2009), 280–281.

9 Benazir Bhutto quoted by ibid., 335.

10 See Simon Walters, "Bhutto email named killers weeks before assassination," *Daily Mail*, Sunday, December 30, 2007.

11 See Robin Wright and Glenn Kessler, "U.S. Brokered Bhutto's Return to Pakistan," *Washington Post*, December 28, 2007.

12 Rashid, *Descent into Chaos*, 377.

13 Rice, *No Higher Honor*, 610–611.

7: The Assassination

1 See Rashid, *Descent into Chaos*, 378.

2 Hamid Karzai quoted by Steve Coll, "Time Bomb: The death of Benazir Bhutto and the unraveling of Pakistan, *New Yorker*, January 28, 2008. http://www.newyorker.com/reporting/2008/01/28/080128 fa_fact_coll.

3 Sherry Rehman, a distinguished journalist, was the federal minister for information and broadcasting (2008–2009). President Asif Ali Zardari named her Pakistan ambassador to the United States on November 23, 2011.

4 See Carlotta Gall, "Musharraf says Bhutto took excessive risks," *New York Times,* January 4, 2008.

5 According to the vehicle's driver, it was Naheed Khan who told Benazir to wave to the crowd, after which Benazir asked for the escape hatch to be opened.

8: Whodunit?

1 See "Transcript: Alleged Al Qaeda Conversation regarding Bhutto Killing," Fox News, December 28, 2007. http://www.foxnews.com/story/2007/12/28/transcript-alleged-al-qaeda-conversation-regarding-bhutto-killing. The full transcript is also fully reproduced in Laura King, "Pakistan lays blame on Taliban," *Baltimore Sun*, December 29, 2007.

2 See "ISI Official Provided Content for BB Murder Press Conference: Cheema," *Dawn*, March 15, 2011.

3 See the executive summary of the report in "Scotland Yard report into the assassination of Benazir Bhutto revealed," CNN.com press release, February 8, 2008.

4 See "Pakistan's Most Wanted: Baitullah Mehsud," *Jane's*, February 12, 2008.

5 A second JIT, led by the Federal Investigative Agency, was constituted in October 2009 to further investigate Bhutto's assassination. This investigation was initiated by the Ministry of the Interior eighteen months after the PPP government presided over by Asif Ali Zardari, Bhutto's widower, had come into power in Pakistan.

6 "Baitullah Mehsud says his bombers are waiting for Benazir Bhutto," *Daily Times*, Pakistan, October 5, 2007.

7 Mehsud's spokesman quoted by Carlota Gall, "Local militants in Pakistan add to Qaeda threat," *New York Times*, December 30, 2007. See, also, "I didn't kill Benazir Bhutto," *Times Now*, December 30, 2007, and Jason Farago "Al-Qaeda ally denies hand in Bhutto killing," *Newser.com*, December 29, 2007. http://www.newser.com/story/15191/al-qaeda-ally-denies-hand-in-bhutto-killing.html.

8 Imran Lalani and Qurat ul ain Siddiqui, "Who is Baitullah Mehsud?", *Dawn*, Pakistan, March 31, 2009.

9 "'We assassinated America's precious asset,' boasts top Al Qaeda commander," *Daily Mail*, London, December 29, 2007.

10 Syed Saleem Shahzad, "Al Qaeda claims Bhutto killing," *Asia Times*, December 27, 2007.

11 Joby Warrick, "CIA places blame for Bhutto Assassination," *Washington Post*, January 18, 2008.

12 See Bruce Riedel, "Mumbai Terror Attack Group Lashkar e Tayyiba Now More Dangerous than Al Qaida," *Daily Beast*, July 1, 2012. See also Jayshree Bajoria, "Lashkar-e-Taiba," Council on Foreign Relations, January 14, 2010.

13 See the report by Mark Mazzetti, Scott Shane, and Alissa Rubin, "A Brutal Afghan Clan Bedevils the U.S.: Haqqani Crime Empire,

an Islamist Force Is Seen as Pakistan's Proxy," *New York Times*, September 25, 2011, A1–A14.

14 See declarations by General Pasha quoted by Salman Masood, "Pakistani Politicians Reject Mullen's Charges," *New York Times*, September 30, 2011, A10.

15 Charlie Wilson quoted in Emma Graham-Harrison, "Haqqani network is considered most ruthless branch of Afghan insurgency," *Guardian*, September 7, 2012.

16 Benazir Bhutto quoted by Steve Coll, "Time Bomb: The death of Benazir and the unraveling of Pakistan."

17 See Amir Mir, "'You can name Musharraf as my assassin if I am killed': Benazir" in Sami Hussain Panher (ed.), *Articles Written to Pay Tribute to Mohtarma Benazir Bhutto*, http://www.bhutto.org, 2008.

18 Hassan Abbas, *Pakistan's Drift into Extremism,* 134.

19 Gul quoted by Loudon, "Who Killed Benazir?," 4.

20 Robert Novak, "Rigging Pakistan's Election?," *Washington Post*, December 3, 2007, A17.

21 See Owen Bennet-Jones, "Questions Concerning the Murder of Benazir Bhutto," *London Review of Books*, 6–10.

22 Benazir Bhutto quoted by Declan Walsh, "Bhutto's return sparks assassination fears," *Guardian*, Sunday, October 14, 2007.

23 See Anatol Lieven, "Understanding Pakistan's Military," ISN, Swiss Federal Institute of Technology, Zurich, August 12, 2010, 1.

24 See the debate in Ashley J. Tellis, Frederic Grare, and Robert Boggs, *Reforming Pakistan's Intelligence Agencies*, Carnegie Endowment for International Peace (Washington, DC: Federal News Service, March 11, 2009).

25 See Hassan Abbas, *Pakistan's Drift into Extremism,* 255.

26 Lieutenant General Asad Durrani, "ISI: An Exceptional Secret Service," Canarytrap.in, August 22, 2011. http://www.canarytrap.in/2011/08/22/isi-an-exceptional-secret-service/.

27 Ibid., 5.

28 "UN Commission Not Allowed Access to Army: Rehman Malik," *Nation*, Pakistan, January 4, 2010.

29 "UN Commission Not Allowed Access to Army: Malik," *News International*, Pakistan, January 4, 2010.

30 President Zardari apparently resisted the restoration of Chaudhry because he feared the political reopening of corruption charges against him under the chief judge and because he considered the judge too close to the opposition. See Zahid Hussain and Matthew Rosenberg, "Pakistan Military Chief Tries to Mediate Standoff," *Wall Street Journal*, March 14–15, 2009, A5.

31 In 2010 the only Pakistani in the same *Time*'s list of one hundred most influential people was the director general of the ISI, General Ahmed Pasha.

32 See Syed Irfan Raza, "UN Probe Team Chief meets Kayani," *Dawn*, February 26, 2010, 1.

33 Richard Elias and Jeremy Watson, "Bhutto murder blamed on Pakistan agents," *Scotland on Sunday*, December 30, 2007.

34 Ahmed Rashid reported this conversation in an interview he had with Karzai. See Rashid, *Descent into Chaos*, 378.

35 Benazir Bhutto quoted by Steve Coll, "Time Bomb," *New Yorker*.

36 See Declan Walsh, "Court Challenges Put Unusual Spotlight on Pakistani Spy Agency," *New York Times*, February 7, 2012, A4–A8, and Declan Walsh and Salmon Masood, "Turmoil in Pakistan as Prime Minister Is Indicted in Contempt Charge," *New York Times*, February 14, 2012, A4–A10.

37 See Carlotta Gall, "Pakistani Military Still Cultivates Militant Groups, a Former Fighter Says," *New York Times*, July 4, 2011, A4.

38 Durrani, "ISI: An Exceptional Secret Service," 3.

39 See Loudon, "Who Killed Benazir?," 4.

40 "Email to Be Used Only 'if I Am Killed,'" *Dawn*, Pakistan, Saturday, December 29, 2007, and "Bhutto Said She'd Blame Musharraf if Killed," CNN.com, December 28, 2007. http://edition.cnn.com/2007/WORLD/asiapcf/12/27/bhutto.security/

41 Musharraf quoted by Lally Weymouth in "Two Leaders, on a Collision Course," interviews with Benazir Bhutto and Pervez Musharraf, *Newsweek* and *The Daily Beast*, December 14, 2007. http://www.thedailybeast.com/newsweek/2007/12/14/two-leaders-on-a-collision-course.html.

42 See Shamim-ur-Rahman, "PPP Letter Seeks UN Investigation Commission," *Dawn*, January 17, 2008.

43 Senator Biden quoted in Carlotta Gall, "Local militants in Pakistan add to Qaeda threat."

44 See Christina Lamb, "Who Murdered Benazir Bhutto?," *Sunday Times*, London, May 2, 2010.

45 See Suskind, *The Way of the World*, 268.

46 Haroon quoted by Bloomberg cable, "Pakistan Unlikely to Act on Bhutto Report, UN Envoy Haroon Says," Businessweek.com, April 16, 2010. http://www.businessweek.com/news/2010-04-16/pakistan-unlikely-to-act-on-bhutto-report-un-envoy-haroon-says.html.

9: The Investigation's Repercussions

1 See Saeed Shah, "Bhutto Killing Conspiracy Theorists Feel Vindicated by Hints of State Involvement," *Guardian*, April 16, 2010.

2 Declan Walsh, "Pakistan Police Officers to Be Arrested over Death of Benazir Bhutto," *Guardian*, December 5, 2010.

3 Sabrina Tavernise, "UN's Bhutto Report Says What Pakistanis Already Know about Spy Agency and Army," *New York Times*, April 17, 2010.

4 "Benazir Bhutto's Assassination: Pakistani Murder Mystery," *Economist*, April 16, 2010.

5 Hamid Gul quoted by Mazhar Tufall, "Hamid Gul Says It Is 'Save Zardari Report,'" *News International*, Pakistan, April 17, 2010.

6 "Musharraf Aide Calls UN's Bhutto Report Lies," *Dawn*, April 16, 2010.

7 See A. Kohar, "UN Team Head Heraldo Munoz Is an Old Suicide Bomber," *Pakistani Spectator*, April 19, 2012.

8 See Yousef Nazar, "Dawn Columnist's Spin on BB's Murder," *State of Pakistan*, May 2, 2010.

9 Babar quoted in Saeed Shah and Ewen MacAskill, "Pakistan to launch new inquiry into Benazir Bhutto murder after UN report," *Guardian*, April 16, 2010.

10 See Asim Yasim, "Musharraf Is BB's Killer: PPP," *News International*, April 17, 2010.

11 "Pakistan Welcomes UN Report on Bhutto Assassination," *Dawn*, April 16, 2010.

12 See "Haroon Hails UN Report on Benazir Murder," *Nation*, Pakistan, April 19, 2010.

13 President Zardari quoted by Syed Irfan Raza, "UN Report Has Vindicated PPP: Zardari," *Dawn*, April 17, 2010, 1.

14 "UN Report Has Strengthened Government Hands, Says Zardari," *News International*, May 6, 2010.

15 See "Pak Objects to UN's Benazir Assassination Report," OneIndia News, June 23, 2010.http://m.oneindia.in/news/2010/06/23/pak objects-to-uns-benazir-assassinationreport.html.

16 See declarations in "UN Rejects Pak Objections over Commission's Benazir Murder Report," Thaindian.com, July 14, 2010. http://www.thaindian.com/newsportal/south-asia/un-rejects-pak-objections-over-commissions-benazir-murder-report_100395521.html.

17 Various Pakistani newspapers quoted in "Pak 'Jittery' over UN Response to Qureshi's Objections on BB Murder Probe," Thaindian.com, July 15, 2010. http://www.thaindian.com/newsportal/south-asia/pak-jittery-over-un-response-to-qureshis-objections-on-bb-murder-probe_100396111.html.

18 See "Benazir Bhutto assassination: 'Pakistan keeping UN letter under wraps'," Zeenews.com, December 28, 2012. http://zeenews.india.com/print.aspx?nid=819328.

19 *Dawn* and others quoted in "Pak Military Forced Government to Record Protest with UN on Benazir Murder Report," Thaindian.com, December 25, 2010. http://www.thaindian.com/newsportal

/south-asia/pak-military-forced-govt-to-record-protest-with-un-on-benazir-murder-report_10047911.html.

20 "Statement attributable to the Spokesperson of the Secretary-General," New York, March 30, 2010.

21 See Foreign Minister Qureshi quoted by Mariana Baabar, "UN, Pakistan at odds over Benazir murder report," *News International*, Friday, April 2, 2010.

22 See Sikander Shaheen, "Government seeking further extension," *Nation*, Pakistan, April 6, 2010, 1.

23 UN spokesperson in Pakistan quoted by "UN delays Benazir murder report at Zardari's request," *News International,* Pakistan, March 31, 2010.

24 Musharraf had told Benazir on one occasion, after the leader of Dubai had contacted him about the threats to her, that she should believe the UAE ruler if she didn't trust him.

25 "ISI's Top Secret Letter Unfolds New Dimension of BB Murder Case," *Dawn*, December 26, 2011. Reportedly, when Malik received this threat information, he wrote a three-page letter to Secretary Kamal Shah requesting enhanced security for Benazir.

26 See "Former Prime Minister Bhutto's Assassination Was Part of a Conspiracy: FIA," *Dawn,* November 16, 2010, 3.

27 Ibid., 2.

28 Shakeel Anjum, "FCC Literally Trashes UN Report on BB Murder," *News International*, May 8, 2010, 1, 8.

29 Saud Aziz quoted by "Police Officers Defend Washing the BB Crime Scene," *News International*, May 5, 2010.

30 Rehman Malik quoted by "Malik Says UN Report Didn't Expose BB Killers," *News International*, April 28, 2010, 1.

31 See "Osama Involved in Benazir Murder: Rehman Malik," NDTV.com, June 22, 2011.

32 See Andrew Buncombe, "Pakistani Interior Minister 'to Reveal Benazir Bhutto Killers in Book,'" *Independent*, December 4, 2012.

33 President Zardari quoted in "Those given refuge 30 years ago killed BB: Zardari," *News International*, April 28, 2010, 1.

34 Abdul Qayyum Khan Jatoi quoted by "Pakistani Minister Resigns After Criticizing the Army," *Washington Times*, September 26, 2010.

35 See "BB Case: ISI and MI Officials to Be Grilled," *News International*, December 23, 2010.

36 See Walsh, "Pakistan Police Officers to Be Arrested."

37 See "Saud Aziz, Khurram Shahzad Arrested in Benazir Case," *Dawn*, December 22, 2010.

38 "Pakistan: Pervez Musharraf 'Accused' over Bhutto Murder," BBC News, February 7, 2011.

39 Quoted by Mehreen Zahra-Malik, "Prosecutor in Bhutto assassination case shot dead: police," Reuters, May 3, 2013. www.reuters.com/assets/print?aid=USBRE94205R20130503. An Al Qaida militant was arrested as one of the alleged attackers (see "Al Qaeda Activist Arrested in Murder of Benezir Base Proseccutor," *Dawn*, June 14, 2013).

40 Fawad Chaudhry quoted by "Musharraf Will Not Comply with Warrant: Spokesman," *Dawn*, February 12, 2011.

41 See Rauf Klasra, "BB Assassination Probe: 'Murder Plot Hatched at Brigadier's Home,'" *Express Tribune*, January 14, 2011. http://tribune.com.pk/story/97269/benazir-bhutto-assassination-probe-murder-plot-hatched-at-brigadiers-home/.

42 See "Bhutto Murder: Pakistan Police and Taliban Charge," BBC News, November 5, 2011. Also, "Pakistan Indicts 7 in Bhutto Assassination," *New York Times*, November 5, 2011.

43 See "Malik Says 27 Terrorist Groups Involved in Benazir's Murder," *Dawn*, February 21, 2012. Shortly thereafter, in mid-April, the Supreme Court advised Minister Malik to quit public office in order to conduct a new transparent and influence-free investigation of the crime, considering that the previous one had not included Minister Malik as a suspect.

44 For a summary of the FIA report, see Asad Kharal, "Benazir Bhutto Assassination Case: JIT Complete Report," *Express Tribune*, Febru-

ary 21, 2012. http://tribune.com.pk/story/339661/benazir-bhutto-assassination-case-jit-complete-report/.

45 Musharraf quoted by Adam Gabbatt, "Pervez Musharraf Vows to Return to 'Suffering' Pakistan during Visit to US," *Guardian*, July 1, 2012.

46 Salman Masood, "Musharraf greeted in Pakistan by threats and small crowds," *New York Times*, March 24, 2013.

47 See "Musharraf facing petitions galore," *Dawn*, March 28, 2013.

48 See "A Trial without an End," *Dawn*, December 27, 2012. At the fifth anniversary of Benazir's murder, the federal minister for information and broadcasting said that one of Bhutto's suspected assassins had just been killed in a drone strike, while the "remaining accused languished in jail." "Benazir's Killer Died in Drone Attack: Kaira," *Dawn*, December 27, 2012.

49 Bilawal Bhutto Zardari quoted in "Bilawal anointed torch-bearer on BB anniversary," *Dawn*, December 28, 2012.

Epilogue: Reflections on Bhutto, bin Laden, and Pakistan's Ties to the United States

1 Clinton, *My Life*, 798.

2 Ibid., 873. See also Bob Woodward and Thomas Ricks, "CIA Trained Pakistanis to Nab Terrorists but Military Coup Put an End to 1999 Plot," *Washington Post*, October 3, 2001.

3 Rashid, *Descent into Chaos*, 224–225. US assistant secretary of state Karl Inderfurth had delivered a blunt message to the Pakistanis asking them to hand over Zubaydah, but to no avail.

4 US ambassador to Afghanistan Zalmay Khalilzad quoted in Seth G. Jones, *In the Graveyard of Empires: America's War in Afghanistan* (New York: W. W. Norton, 2010), 265–266.

5 See "Pakistani Army Denies Sharing US Report with Bomb Makers," *New York Times*, June 18, 2011, A8.

6 President George W. Bush, "The President's News Conference with President Pervez Musharraf of Pakistan," The White House, September 22, 2006.

7 Rashid, *Descent into Chaos*, 407.

8 See Special Report: Peter Bergen, "The Last days of Osama bin Laden," and Graham Allison, "How it went down," *Time* 179, no. 18 (May 7, 2012): 26–41.

9 See Nicholas Schmidle, "Getting Bin Laden," *New Yorker*, August 8, 2011. See also Marc Ambinder and D. B. Grady, "The Story of How U.S. Special Forces Infiltrated Pakistan," *Atlantic*, February 16, 2012.

10 Mark Mazzetti, "Signs that Bin Laden Weighed Seeking Pakistani Protection," *New York Times*, May 27, 2011, A7.

11 See Baqir Sajjad Syed, "'Culpable negligence, incompetence at all levels of government': report," *Dawn*, July 9, 2013.

12 Dr. Afridi was sentenced to thirty-three years in prison and a fine equivalent to about $3,500. See Ibrahim Shinwari and Jibran Ahmed, "Pakistani Doctor Jailed for Helping CIA Find Bin Laden," Reuters.com, May 23, 2012.

13 This incident strained CIA-ISI relations further as, initially, the CIA denied that Davis was an agency employee. See Mark Mazzetti, "Pakistan's Public Enemy," *New York Times Magazine*, April 9, 2013, 30–41.

14 See David Sanger and Eric Schmitt, "White House Assails Pakistan Effort on Militants," *New York Times*, April 6, 2011, A6. See also "Pakistan and US in Patch-Up Efforts," *Dawn*, April 8, 2011, 2.

15 Admiral Mullen quoted by "Haqqani network is a 'veritable arm' of ISI: Mullen", *Dawn*, September 22, 2011.

16 See Masood, "Pakistani Politicians Reject Mullen's Charges," A10.

17 President Obama quoted by Rick Gladstone, "Obama Warns Pakistanis on Militants," *New York Times*, October 7, 2011, A4.

18 See Mansoor Ijaz, "It Is Time to Take on Pakistan's Radical Jihadist Spies," *Financial Times*, October 11, 2011, 9.

19 See Shaiq Hussain, "Ex-Envoy Husain Haqqani Was behind Memo Seeking US Help, Pakistani Probe Finds," *Washington Post*, June 12, 2012.

20 See Eric Schmidt and Salman Masood, "Pakistani Strains Prompt Leader to Race Home," *New York Times*, December 19, 2011, A5.

21 See Gilani quoted by Salman Masood, "Pakistani Premier Warns of Plotting by Military," *New York Times*, December 23, 2011, A13.

22 See Kayani quoted by Salman Masood and Matthew Rosenbert, "As Rumors Buzz, Pakistan's Military Denies Talk of a Coup," *New York Times*, December 24, 2011, A4.

23 In September 2010, after two Pakistani paramilitary soldiers were killed in a similar border clash, Pakistan closed the land route through its territory that NATO uses to supply its forces in Afghanistan for more than a week.

24 See Eric Schmitt and David Sanger, "US Seeks Aid from Pakistan in Peace Effort," *New York Times*, October 31, 2011, A1, and Alissa Rubin, "Former Taliban Officials Say US Talks Started," *New York Times*, January 29, 2012, A9.

25 Arif Rafiq, "The Emergence of the Difa-e-Pakistan Islamist Coalition," *CTC Sentinel*, Combating Terrorism Center, March 22, 2012. Hafiz Saeed, a main proponent of the DPC and the head of a banned charity linked to Lashkar-e-Taiba, is sought by the United States, which offered a $10 million reward for information leading to his arrest (the Pakistani government and the opposition strongly criticized the announced reward). However, Saeed is not in hiding, as he gave a press conference in mid-2012 taunting US authorities to come and get him. See Joshua Keating, "Five People Who Are Not in Jail in Pakistan," *Foreign Policy*, May 23, 2012.

26 Leon Panetta quoted by "Leon Panetta: US Officials Reaching the Limits of Our Patience with Pakistan," *Huffington Post*, June 6, 2012. http://www.huffingtonpost.com/2010/06/07/leon-paneta-pakistan-patience_n_1577118.htm.

27 See Byron Tau, "Clinton Apologizes to Pakistan, Announces Supply Route Deal," *Politico*, July 3, 2012. http://www.politico.com/politico44/2012/07/clinton-apologizes-to-pakistan-announces-supply-route-127966.html. It had been discussed that Pakistan was demanding an increase in transit taxes from $250 per truck to $5,000 per truck, which US Defense Secretary Panetta had described as "price gouging."

28 Jane Perlez, "The Fight over How to End a War," *New York Times*, October 20, 2011, A14.

29 See Yogesh Joshi, "Understanding Pakistan's Nuclear Rationale," ISN, Swiss Federal Institute of Technology, Zurich, May 26, 2011.

30 See Farhan Bokhari and Kathrin Hille, "Pakistan Solicits China to Build Naval Base at South-Western Port," *Financial Times*, May 23, 2011, 1. See also Harsh V. Pant, "China and Pakistan," ISN, Swiss Federal Institute of Technology, Zurich, June 20, 2011.

31 Asif Ali Zardari, "The Frontier against Terrorism," *Washington Post*, June 22, 2009.

32 The Kerry-Lugar-Berman Act, signed by President Obama in October 2009, promised $7.5 billion in nonmilitary aid over five years. It requires the secretary of state to certify that Pakistan is cooperating in thwarting nuclear proliferation and terrorism in Afghanistan and elsewhere. See "State of Vulnerability," *Economist*, February 13, 2012. Since 9/11, Pakistan has received more than $20 billion in military and development assistance, not counting covert funds.

33 See Pir Zubair Shah, "My Drone War," *Foreign Policy*, March–April 2012, 6. http://www.foreignpolicy.com/articles/2012/02/27/my_drone_war.

34 See Mark Mazzetti, "A secret deal on drones, sealed in blood," *New York Times*, April 7, 2013, A1 and A8.

35 Musharraf cited by ibid, A8.

36 See "UN official says US drones breach Pakistan's sovereignty," *New York Times*, March 16, 2013, A5.

37 See Salman Masood, "NATO Supply Trucks from Pakistan Resume Trek to Afghanistan," *New York Times*, July 5, 2012, A4. See also Pew Research Center, "Global Attitudes Project: Global Opinion of Obama Slips, International Policies Faulted," Wednesday, June 13, 2012.

38 The Pakistan Penal Code forbids blasphemy against any recognized religion, providing penalties that range from fines to death. Pakistan protects Islamic authority, given that Islam is the state religion, according to the constitution. Numerous people accused of blasphemy have gone into hiding or have left the country after being subjected to harassment or attacks. The calls for reform of the code

to limit abuse and restrictions on freedom of expression have been strongly resisted by Islamic parties and have not progressed. Twitter, Facebook, and the Internet in general are monitored by the authorities and in some instances have been blocked for contents allegedly offensive to Muslims.

39 See Declan Walsh and Zia ur-Rehman, "Taliban terrorize Karachi as the new gang in town," *New York Times*, March 29, 2013, A1 and A3.

40 The army also indirectly criticized Chaudhry when army chief Kayani warned that "no individual or institution has the monopoly to decide what is right or wrong in defining the ultimate national interest," to which the judge replied that the court's paramount authority was enshrined in the constitution. (See Salman Masood, "Top Pakistani Generals and Judges Trade Barbs," *New York Times*, November 6, 2012, A7.) The image of Pakistan's Chief Justice Chaudhry was somewhat tarnished when his court brushed aside accusations from a billionaire who testified that he had given Chaudhry's thirty-two-year-old son $3.7 million in bribes and bankrolled luxury vacations in London and Monte Carlo for the son and his wife.

41 In September 2012, Pakistan and India signed a visa agreement easing restrictions for travelers, a significant step toward normalizing relations. Moreover, bilateral trade between the two countries has jumped from $300 million in 2004 to $2.7 billion in 2011. See Salman Masood, "India and Pakistan Sign Visa Agreement, Easing Travel," *New York Times*, September 9, 2012, A12.

42 Ironically, in August 2012, neighbor and rival India was affected by a major power blackout that left 670 million people without electricity.

43 See Roman Muzaleosky, "Enhancing Pakistan's Energy Security," ISN, Swiss Federal Institute of Technology Zurich, July 18, 2011.

44 The 2012 United Nations Development Programme (UNDP) Human Development Index (HDI) noted an improving trend in the nation's HDI value since 1980. However, Pakistan ranks among the countries with Low Human Development, occupying the number 146 position among 186 countries. (See UNDP, *The Rise of the South*, Human Development Report 2013, New York, 2013, 143 and 150.) Poverty incidence decreased from 34.5 percent in 2000–

2001 to 22.3 percent in 2005–2006, the latest year for which official figures are available. (See Executive Board of the UNDP, the UNFPA, and the UNOPS, "Draft Common Country Program for Pakistan and the UNDP Results and Resources Framework, 2013–2017," DP/DCCP/PAK/1, July 30, 2012, 3.)

45 See Salma Siddiqui, "Survival of the Richest," ISN, Swiss Federal Institute of Technology Zurich, October 6, 2010.

46 Mian Muhammad Mansha, interview by Henny Sender, "There Is a Lot of Anger in Pakistan," *Financial Times*, August 11–12, 2012, 3.

47 "UK aid to Pakistan should stop unless taxes rise, MPs say," Channel4.com, April 4, 2013. http://www.channel4.com/news/uk-aid-to-pakistan-should-stop-unless-taxes-rise-mps-say.

48 Benazir Bhutto, *Reconciliation*, 306.

Index

Page numbers in *italics* refer to illustrations.

Adarsh 244
29-4-14 ME